The ARTHRITIS SOLUTION
for DOGS

ALSO AVAILABLE
FROM THE NATURAL VET™

The Allergy Solution for Dogs
The Arthritis Solution for Dogs

THE *Natural Vet* SERIES

The ARTHRITIS SOLUTION for DOGS

—————— • ——————

NATURAL AND CONVENTIONAL
THERAPIES TO EASE PAIN AND
ENHANCE YOUR DOG'S QUALITY OF LIFE

Shawn Messonnier, D.V.M.

PRIMA PETS
AN IMPRINT OF PRIMA PUBLISHING
3000 LAVA RIDGE COURT • ROSEVILLE, CALIFORNIA 95661
(800) 632-8676 • WWW.PRIMALIFESTYLES.COM

DISCLAIMER: While the Publisher and the author have designed this book to provide up-to-date information in regard to the subject matter covered, readers should be aware that medical information is constantly evolving. The information presented herein is of a general nature and is not intended as a substitute for professional medical advice. Readers should consult with a qualified veterinarian for specific instructions on the treatment and care of their pet. The author and Prima Publishing shall have neither liability nor responsibility to any person or entity with respect to any loss, damage, or injury caused or alleged to be caused directly or indirectly by the information contained in this book.

THE NATURAL VET series and PRIMA PETS are trademarks of Prima Communications, Inc. The Prima colophon is a trademark of Prima Communications Inc., registered with the United States Patent and Trademark Office.

All products mentioned in this book are trademarks of their respective companies.

Library of Congress Cataloging-in-Publication Data
Messonnier, Shawn.
    The arthritis solution for dogs : natural and conventional therapies to ease pain and enhance your dog's quality of life / Shawn Messonnier.
        ——— p. cm.
    ISBN 0-7615-2622-6
    Dogs—Diseases. 2. Arthritis in animals. I. Title.
    SF992.A77 M47 2000
    636.7'0896722—dc21   00-023000

00 01 02 03 HH 10 9 8 7 6 5 4 3 2 1
Printed in the United States of America

How to Order
Single copies may be ordered from Prima Publishing, 3000 Lava Ridge Court, Roseville, CA 95661; telephone (800) 632-8676 ext. 4444. Quantity discounts are also available. On your letterhead, include information concerning the intended use of the books and the number of books you wish to purchase.

Visit us online at www.primalifestyles.com

CONTENTS

Foreword by Robert J. Silver, D.V.M., M.S.   vi
Preface   ix
Acknowledgments   xi
Introduction   xii

1. Understanding Arthritis   1

2. Not Arthritis, But Something Else   11

3. What Can I Expect at My Veterinary Visit?   39

4. Conventional Treatments for Arthritis   57

5. Complementary Therapies for Arthritis   87

6. Additional Complementary Therapies   125

7. Diet and Arthritis   147

8. Exercise and Physical Therapy for Your Pet   171

9. Arthritis Prevention   181

10. Tying It All Together   201

Bibliography   205
Index   211

FOREWORD

HE PAST FIVE years have seen a huge outpouring of interest by pet owners and veterinarians about the practice of holistic veterinary medicine. This burgeoning interest in alternative healthcare for animals follows the similar trend of interest that has been been growing just as rapidly in alternative health care for humans. Just as people have been able to experience the benefits first-hand of holistic and natural approaches to their own health, they naturally want to convey these same benefits to their four-legged family members.

If you are looking for a book that can help you expand your knowledge base about natural therapies for your pets, then you need look no further. This very complete and well-written book by Dr. Shawn Messonnier will provide you with a well-balanced approach to keeping your pets healthy. I agree with his perspective that holistic veterinary health care is an integration of the best of conventional medicine and the best of alternative medicine. Messonnier does not "throw the baby out with the bath water" in promoting this perspective, rather he promotes a commonsense, integrated, and complementary approach to animal health care.

It's the job of the holistic veterinarian to understand more about the context of their animal patient in its home environment. Healthy family interactions play a large role in promoting the health and wellness of all the family members (including the pets). Dysfunctional family dynamics can likewise promote illness and chronic disease in our pets. To better promote the health of the animal and the family that it lives with, the holistic veterinarian, as part of this holistic process, tries to make a better "fit" between the animal and its family. This healthier connection with the family will contribute to optimal health and happiness within the family unit.

Holistic veterinarians try to follow the Hippocratic Oath which states:"Above All, Do No Harm." Holistic vets try to avoid the unnecessary use of drugs and surgeries if they are not needed for the animal's health. Vaccinations, although helpful in preventing certain epidemic and epizootic diseases, may not be necessary every year. (Only the rabies vaccine is required by law in every state.) In fact, vaccinations may even be harmful if given that frequently. Duration of immunity studies are now being completed which are demonstrating that vaccinations given early in the life of the animal (by 12 weeks of age) may have a protectiveness that lasts for many, many years, if not for the life of the animal. And annual administration of vaccinations has been implicated in a number of degenerative diseases, including cancer and auto-immune disease.

Another commonly held assumption that holistic veterinarians question includes the wisdom of feeding nothing but commercial dog food for the life of the pet. It has been recognized in recent years that commercial pet foods are overly processed, laden with adulterants, and made from poor quality raw materials, much of which have been condemned for human consumption. In own my clinical practice of 18 years, I have found no greater healing tool for my patients than to take them off the commercial diet and switch them (slowly and gradually!) to a fresh, wholesome (and in many cases) raw food diet. I have seen no evidence of bacterial contamination in the undercooked food leading to bacterial enteritis. It is important to gradually make the switch to the new food. But 99 percent of all animals will adapt very well to the dietary improvement.

This collection of informational books, THE NATURAL VET™ series by Dr. Shawn Messonnier, will be a valuable addition to the natural health care section of your library, whether you are a "pet parent" wanting to give your four-legged family member a more natural upbringing or a veterinarian wanting to learn more about these useful and emerging therapies. As a veterinarian, I have found that my clients have appreciated my adding these new "natural" tools to my practice bag. We supply a wide variety of excellent books on natural therapies for animals at our animal wellness center. THE NATURAL VET™ series will join the many other fine books available at my veterinary clinic.

Robert J. Silver, D.V.M, M.S.

PREFACE

I AM A CONVENTIONAL doctor by training, an Aggie from the Lone Star State. I graduated in 1987 from Texas A&M University with a doctorate of veterinary medicine, and in 1991 opened Paws & Claws Animal Hospital, the first referral hospital for dogs, cats, and exotic pets in Plano, Texas.

After using conventional treatments for several years, I became convinced that many pets that were not improving with lifelong use of conventional medications might improve if some type of alternative was available. This desire to improve the quality of my patients' lives led me to become adept at treating pets with a variety of complementary therapies. Due to the success of this idea, I created the Acupuncture and Holistic Animal Health Care Center, the only hospital in the area to offer both conventional and complementary therapies for dogs and cats.

Now, in addition to practicing medicine, I spread the word of holistic health care for pets as a regular columnist for the *Dallas Morning News* and the *Wylie News*. For two years, I hosted Fox Television's "4 Your Pets" pet-care show. I serve on the board of the prestigious international journal, *Veterinary Forum,* and I am also founder and editor-in-chief of *Exotic Pet Practice,* the only monthly international publication devoted to the care of exotic pets. Each month I reach over half a million pet owners as the holistic columnist for both *Dog Fancy* and *Cat Fancy* magazines. I also serve as a consultant to Our Pets, a leading manufacturer of natural pet products, and I am the holistic veterinarian for www.planetpets.com.

As a speaker, consultant, and writer, I teach veterinarians and pet owners around the world how holistic methods can reduce the cost of veterinary care and help pets live longer, healthier lives. I challenge everyone I work with to be the best they can be and to rise above any challenges they may face, and I am committed to providing the best health care for my patients.

This book, *The Arthritis Solution for Dogs,* is part of a brand-new series of health guides called THE NATURAL VET™. With this exciting project I hope to show you ways to care for your pets using safe, natural, alternative treatments for a variety of medical conditions.

ACKNOWLEDGMENTS

The *Arthritis Solution for Dogs* is the first book in the THE NATURAL VET™ series. I am happy to be working with the fine folks at Prima Publishing, including my editors, Lorna Eby and Libby Larson, and publisher, Ben Dominitz. Their vision and acceptance of my idea for a holistic series was instrumental in getting this book into your hands.

A big thanks to all holistic doctors for sharing their ideas with me and with the profession through their books and clinical articles. Your desire to do what is best for our pets is appreciated by all.

A special thanks to Dr. Christina Chambreau for her help with the section on homeopathy.

Drs. Joseph Kandel and David Sudderth wrote *The Arthritis Solution* (for people). Their great book served as a guide and template for the books in THE NATURAL VET™ series. Thank you!

Thank you to God for the talent and drive to do all I desire.

Finally, as always, a big "thanks, hugs, and kisses" to Sandy and Erica. Your support means a lot.

INTRODUCTION

ONE WEDNESDAY, MY day began with a visit from one of my favorite pet clients, Jake, a 10-year-old Labrador retriever. His owner told me that Jake seemed to be having more difficulty getting around. This is a common complaint from owners of older, large breed dogs, many of which do exhibit varying degrees of lameness as they age. The cause is often something relatively simple—hip dysplasia or arthritis, for example. Sometimes the culprit is more sinister—cancer or degeneration of the spinal nerves.

To help determine the cause of Jake's lameness, we sedated him and took radiographs (x-rays) of his hips and spine. In Jake's case, these simple radiographs showed mild hip dysplasia with secondary arthritis. Because Jake's owner was holistic-minded and preferred natural therapies to medications when possible, I started Jake on a regimen of fatty acids and nutritional supplements containing glucosamine and chondroitin. Within a few weeks he was moving around much better, and would never experience any of the side effects that can appear in pets that receive prescribed chronic therapy with anti-arthritic medications.

Lameness due to arthritis is a very common problem in older dogs. While younger dogs can also become lame from a variety of causes (just as younger people can), aging pets in particular tend to show the wear and tear of activity in their joints as they age. Many of these older dogs have lived with joint instability—frequently caused by hip dysplasia or spinal problems—for a number of years, often without their owners knowing the pet had any underlying problems.

This book will explore the most common treatment options available for the arthritic dog so that you, the pet's owner, can work with your veterinarian to determine the best course of action. This book is not meant to replace a visit to a qualified veterinary clinic. In fact, I encourage you to insist that your dog receive proper diagnosis.

Your goal as a pet owner is simple: Do what is in the best interest of your pet. If that includes conventional therapies such as surgery and drug therapy, so be it. If your dog is better treated with a complementary therapy such as herbal medicine, homeopathy, or acupuncture (all of which you will hear about in later chapters), that's great too. Many of my canine patients benefit from a combination of approaches that I call "holistic pet care," which I define simply as keeping our minds open to doing whatever is in the best interests of our four-legged friends.

> Your goal as a pet owner is simple: Do what is in the best interest of your pet.

When it comes to treating your arthritic dog, you have a number of options. The reason I suggest so many options is that no one "best" solution exists for every dog's problem. In my private practice I discuss my philosophy—that each pet is an individual, and must be treated as such—with owners right from the start. I explain that what worked for the last arthritic dog I treated may not work for their pet. Each owner is unique as well; all have different wants and budgets for the pet. Some owners want to do everything possible for their pet—money is no object, and they have the time and interest plus a cooperative animal that will allow us to experiment with a number of unique treatments. Other people opt for a bit less; they may not mind giving their pet conventional medications such as corticosteroids or non-steroidal anti-inflammatory drugs for the long haul or are uncomfortable with more complementary treatments. Still others never want any medications and choose more natural complementary therapies.

> No one "best" solution exists for every dog's problem.

In my practice, I often use a conventional therapy when it is in that pet's best interest, but also supplement treatment with a few well-chosen complementary therapies to provide what I call "holistic" pet care.

UNDERSTAND YOUR TREATMENT OPTIONS

COMPLEMENTARY THERAPY MEANS any therapy that is an alternative to conventional medical treatment. This would include treatments such as homeopathy, acupuncture, herbal medicine, and nutritional medicine, to name a few common ones. The term complementary therapy is often used interchangeably with alternative therapy, but this usage is not quite accurate. "Alternative" implies "something other than." The term "complementary therapy" (also called integrative therapy) implies that the chosen treatment is "complementing" the standard treatment, but not necessarily replacing it. Since most holistic doctors are open-minded to both forms of treatment, the preferred term "complementary therapy" means that our treatment, such as acupuncture or homeopathy, is used in conjunction with and complements the traditional medical therapy that may be prescribed. "Natural care" refers to using treatments other than traditional drug therapies.

To be open to doing what is in the pet's best interest, doctor and pet owners alike must develop what I call a "holistic mindset." Remember that "holistic care" refers to a way of thinking. The holistic doctor and owner view the dog in its entirety, rather than just focusing on one set of problems or signs and symptoms.

> The holistic doctor and owner view the dog in its entirety, rather than just focusing on one set of problems or signs and symptoms.

The goal of holistic care is disease prevention. As a holistic doctor, I prefer to "treat the pet" rather than "treat a disease" (at best) or "treat signs and symptoms" (at worst). Those who adopt the holistic mindset consider *all* options, then choose those that are in the pet's best interest.

By changing our thought processes to see pet care in a more holistic way, we can all benefit, especially our pets. Having a holistic attitude means that doctors and owners refuse to focus specifically on the problem at hand, but instead focus on total wellness for the pet. Ultimately the pet will benefit from this way of care.

The truly holistic view, which most pet owners desire, involves looking at all options and choosing those that work best with the fewest side effects. It means looking at healing the entire pet, rather than simply covering up symptoms. Holistic doesn't only involve complementary therapies. If the goal of conventional drug therapy in treating canine arthritis is to help the dog become healthier overall, rather than to simply feel better, it can become part of the holistic approach.

A conventional doctor by training, I know that conventional therapies work well for a number of dogs. Drugs such as corticosteroids and non-steroidal anti-inflammatory medications (NSAIDs) are not by nature harmful when used correctly. If your dog is particularly difficult to medicate, you may choose to treat your arthritic dog "as needed" with long-acting injectable corticosteroids. However, to do the best, most natural, and holistic thing for the pet, you would be wise to consider other options before resigning your pet to chronic drug therapy.

I believe that offering a combination of both conventional and complementary therapies gives arthritic dogs the best of both worlds. By knowing the pros and cons of every type of medical care, as a dog owner, you too can work with your veterinarian to pick the therapies that you find most comfortable, and that are most beneficial to your dog.

The goal of this book is to help you become an informed consumer of veterinary information so that you can be an active participant in the care of your lame dog. By reading about the possible causes of lameness and what you can expect at a veterinary visit, you will know what symptoms to look for in your dog and what questions to ask your dog's doctor so your pet receives a proper diagnosis. By understanding your options for treating arthritis—conventional therapies and complementary therapies—you will be able to establish a holistic treatment approach that best serves your pet.

· 1 ·

Understanding
Arthritis

ARTHRITIS, OR MORE correctly osteoarthritis or degenerative joint disease (DJD), is a common condition in older dogs.

In some cases, this disease can be prevented if recognized early enough and treated holistically through both conventional and complementary therapies. Once your dog is properly diagnosed, you will want to seek an approach that minimizes the dog's pain and counteracts the effects of the inflammation, and, if possible, also slows the progression of the arthritis and actually helps to heal.

GET A PROPER DIAGNOSIS

BECAUSE LAMENESS CAUSED by osteoarthritis is commonly found in older pets, and because many doctors are uncomfortable treating geriatric pets, older dogs are often ignored and not treated properly. Many veterinarians, instead of performing diagnostic testing to determine the cause and the severity of the problem, and instead of searching for the least harmful treatment options, just try to make these pets comfortable for whatever time the pet has left. These pets are often treated with corticosteroids or non-steroidal medications without the benefit of a proper diagnosis. While nothing is wrong with making pets comfortable, assuming that geriatric pets with osteoarthritis are on their last legs is unreasonable. Many older pets can look forward to months or years of good quality living when doctors treat them as they would younger pets. There's also no reason for doctors to reach for the "magic shot" of corticosteroids or other potentially harmful medications such as non-steroidal medications if more natural, safer alternatives are available.

> Many older pets can look forward to months or years of good quality living when doctors treat them as they would younger pets.

While conventional therapy for osteoarthritis poses numerous concerns, perhaps the greatest is that many veterinarians prescribe without getting a proper diagnosis. It may be that these doctors don't want owners to have to spend much money on diagnosing their pets' problems. Maybe the doctors simply assume that the pets have arthritis, which they figure is easy enough to treat with corticosteroids or other medications that relieve pain and inflammation, and simply hope the pet doesn't experience serious side effects. These reasons, however, are poor excuses for failing to diagnose and treat the pet correctly. While arthritis is certainly the most common diagnosis in older, lame pets, other more serious conditions can also cause lameness. Bone infections, tumors, injuries, bacterial or fungal bone cysts, bone tumors, fractures, ligamentous injuries (cruciate injuries), and joint instability (hip dysplasia, shoulder dysplasia, elbow dysplasia, and osteochondritis) are among the more common causes. These will be discussed in chapter 2.

It troubles me when I see so many pets that have not received a proper diagnosis (a good number never had *any* diagnostic tests), but have been treated for months or years with potentially harmful therapies. There is simply no excuse for failing to obtain a proper diagnosis prior to treating a pet. Often a simple radiograph, a test any doctor is able to perform, will reveal the cause of the pet's lameness. No decision should be made concerning the long-term care of your dog until you know exactly what's wrong.

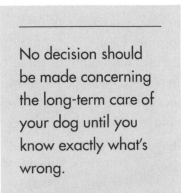

No decision should be made concerning the long-term care of your dog until you know exactly what's wrong.

RESEARCH COMPLEMENTARY THERAPIES

ONE OF THE difficulties in writing a book discussing complementary therapies for pets is trying to find any good research showing that any of these therapies actually work. Unlike the volumes of research data on conventional drug therapies, there just isn't as much research behind many complementary therapies. The basic reason for this is financial. The company doing the study must be prepared to spend a lot of money—often hundreds of thousands and even millions of dollars—to run the kind of double-blind, placebo-controlled study considered the gold standard of research on conventional medicines. In order to spend this large sum of money, the company must first have the money and then also expect to be able to recoup this investment plus a nice profit in the future. Most companies that manufacture complementary therapies do not have this amount of capital. And even if they did, the chance of making enough profit from many of these therapies simply does not exist.

Because many of these therapies cannot be patented, there is no financial incentive to run the study. For example, because simple herbs are common and exist in our environment, they cannot be patented. Neither can other complementary therapies or homeopathic remedies.

Unfortunately, this means that we don't have many good double-blind, placebo-controlled studies to use to back up our recommendations for treating arthritic pets with complementary therapies.

Why are double-blind, placebo-controlled studies considered the gold standard? In this type of study, neither the doctor nor the patient (in this case the pet owner) knows if the treatment being administered is the "active agent" or the placebo. This lack of knowledge on the part of both doctor and owner makes the study "double-blind." Because there are always patients who get better on a placebo, a placebo is always used in this type of study so that the number of pets who respond to the "active agent" can be compared to the number of pets responding to the placebo and the results can be statistically compared.

This kind of study is ideal to "prove" or "disprove" that a certain recommended therapy works, and is always done to get government approval for a new drug. Because most complementary therapies do not have the benefit of this type of study, they are open to a lot of criticism from "conventional doctors."

The evidence I consider for the complementary therapies I use and recommend often comes from my own experience and the experience of other established holistic veterinarians. Namely, I know that they work because they have been used for years and I can see the results. While these experiences are in no way as good as the double-blind, placebo-controlled studies, often they are all that is available. Many of the recommended therapies in *The Arthritis Solution for Dogs* fall into this category.

The final source of my research on complementary therapies for arthritic pets is extrapolation from the human literature. In many instances throughout this book I mention approaches that have been suggested to work or have been proven to work in people. While there are no guarantees nor can we automatically extrapolate from the human literature and apply it to pets, if a treatment works for people it may work for pets. Therefore I have included these therapy options for you to discuss with your doctor.

So the bottom line is this: Before you condemn your dog to chronic conventional drug therapy, get a proper diagnosis. If you are interested in holistic pet care, find a veterinarian who shares this mindset. Every doctor can refer cases he or she is uncomfortable handling.

WHERE ARTHRITIS STRIKES

ARTHRITIS TECHNICALLY MEANS "inflammation of the joint." Arthritis, in dogs and people, is an inflammatory disease characterized by swelling, stiffness, and pain. When treating pets that have arthritis, our therapy must seek to counteract the effects of inflammation. Ideally, it would also

A CLOSER LOOK

The components of the joint include the bones of the joint, ligaments from surrounding muscles that cross the joint space and attach to the bones, and the joint capsule that encloses the joint. The joint capsule contains a thick protective outer layer and a thin inner layer called the synovial membrane. The synovial membrane contains blood vessels and nerves and produces synovial fluid.

The end of each bone is covered with cartilage called articular cartilage, which acts as a shock absorber to protect the bone. The articular cartilage lacks blood vessels and nerves, and is dependent upon diffusion of nutrients from a special fluid in the joint called synovial fluid. The synovial fluid lines the joint space, nourishing the cartilage, and acts as a lubricant and shock absorber.

be advantageous if the therapy could slow down the progression of the arthritis or, if possible, actually help the joint to heal. Most conventional therapies do a great job of treating inflammation and pain but rarely help the joint to heal. In many cases, these anti-inflammatory therapies actually cause more cartilage damage as time progresses. Conversely, many complementary therapies not only relieve pain and inflammation but actually supply nutrients to help the cartilage heal and slow down the destructive forces of nature that act to destroy the injured joint. Joints commonly affected with arthritis include the knee, shoulder, ankle, elbow, and most commonly in dogs, the hips. The joints between the vertebrae of the backbone (spine) also commonly develop arthritis. In most dogs, arthritis of the spine does not cause pain or discomfort.

Arthritis results from erosion of the articular cartilage lining the joints. The lack of nerves in the articular cartilage is an important factor in the progression of arthritis. A great amount of damage can occur to the cartilage before the surrounding joint tissues (joint capsule, bones, and ligaments) become inflamed and cause lameness. Because of this, considerable cartilage damage is often present by the time the animal actually feels any pain and shows signs of lameness. Annual screening of the hips and spine, the most common joints affected with osteoarthritis, will allow for early diagnosis and treatment—before irreversible cartilage damage occurs (see sidebar on page 8).

With enough degradation of the cartilage, underlying bone might become damaged, and the animal may refuse to use the affected limb. That's when the dog begins to limp and its owner often seeks medical care. Some pets can still be helped with nutritional therapies to heal the joint, whereas others may have arthritis that is too advanced to actually allow for healing. The earlier the pet is diagnosed, the greater the chance for healing to occur using complementary therapies.

In addition to this general pathway for damage to the joint and its components, there are certainly specific causes of arthritis as well. For example, dogs with hip dysplasia have abnormal hip joints that lead to instability. As the instability progresses, the body attempts to stabilize the joint by forming new bone around the joint. While this sounds like a good idea, unfortunately this new bone does not stabilize the joint but rather causes pain and inflammation. This new

A CLOSER LOOK

The articular cartilage has a unique structure that allows it to handle the stressful loads placed on it as the animal walks and plays. The articular cartilage is made of cartilage cells (the medical term is chondrocytes) and the surrounding tissue called matrix. The major components of this cartilage matrix are a type of protein called collagen, water, and proteoglycans. The proteoglycan molecule is made of a central core of protein with numerous side chains of glycosaminoglycans (GAGS). There are several different proteoglycan molecules in the joint cartilage, including chondroitin sulfate (the predominant GAG in cartilage) and keratan sulfate. Glucosamine, a popular treatment for osteoarthritis, is a precursor chemical necessary for glycosaminoglycan synthesis. As we discuss nutritional treatments of arthritis, it will be important to remember the terms glycosaminoglycan, proteoglycan, and chondroitin sulfate, as some of these treatments attempt to furnish more of these molecules to help the cartilage heal.

As the animal walks and plays, a large amount of stress is placed on all the components of the joint. The stress causes biomechanical and biochemical alterations in the joint to occur. With years of wear and tear on the joints, the cartilage breaks down and arthritis can develop. As wear and tear continues, the cartilage is disrupted and joint instability results. Chondrocytes are not able to synthesize enough of the proteoglycans to help the cartilage heal. As the chondrocytes become degraded, inflammatory chemicals are released causing inflammation and further damaging the cartilage. The inflammatory chemicals also disrupt the proteoglycans.

bone and accompanying inflammation in and around is called arthritis. Dogs with arthritis of the spine develop the new bone and inflammation most likely as a result of degeneration of the intervertebral disks, the cartilage shock absorbers located in between each vertebrae. Regardless of the cause, with time and joint instability, more new bone and inflammation occur. As the arthritis progresses, clinical signs begin to appear.

INFLAMMATION

SINCE INFLAMMATION IS one of the key signs of arthritis and the goal of most therapies for pets with arthritis is to relieve inflammation, it's important for you to understand just what inflammation is and how to relieve this side effect of arthritis. Inflammation is caused by damage to the tissues and cells of the affected body part.

Cell membranes contain chemicals called phospholipids. When the cell membrane is injured, as in the arthritic pet, an enzyme acts on the phospholipids to produce fatty acids including an omega-6 fatty acid called arachidonic acid and an omega-3 fatty acid called eicosapentanoic acid. Further metabolism of the arachidonic acid and eicosapentanoic acid by additional enzymes yields the production of chemicals called eicosanoids. The eicosanoids produced by metabolism of the omega-6 fatty acids tend to be pro-inflammatory and cause inflammation, suppress the immune system, and cause platelets to aggregate and clot. When a tissue is inflamed, the area may be red, painful, tender, and swollen, and the dog will have a loss of function.

While osteoarthritis is the most common cause of lameness in dogs, it is not the exclusive cause. Other common causes are described in the next chapter.

CHAPTER SUMMARY

• Before beginning any treatment for your pet, be sure to get a proper diagnosis.

• The most common cause of lameness in dogs is osteo-arthritis.

• A painful condition, arthritis is medically called osteo-arthritis or degenerative joint disease.

• Osteoarthritis is an inflammation of the joint, found most commonly in dogs in the joint of the hips.

• The sooner the problem is diagnosed, the greater the treatment options.

· 2 ·

Not Arthritis,
But Something Else

MOST OF THE time lameness in dogs is caused by osteoarthritis. As I already mentioned, as your pet ages, the years of wear and tear on his joints lead to destruction of the articular (joint) cartilage and the resulting sign of lameness.

However, other causes—some even more serious than arthritis—lead to lameness. The list that follows is not intended to substitute for a proper diagnosis. It is a tool for you to use to help your veterinarian determine exactly what is causing your dog to go lame once arthritis has been ruled out, or if the treatment for arthritis is not the complete solution to your dog's problem.

An unusual case of misdiagnosis presented itself to me recently. Angus, a 7-year-old male neutered Rottweiler, was referred to me for acupuncture for presumed hip dysplasia. At 149 pounds, I estimated Angus to be approximately 30 to 40 pounds overweight. Recently, Angus showed difficulty moving around. He had been more lethargic beginning about 2 to 3 weeks prior to our visit. Within the previous week, according to his owner, Angus "staggered as if he was drunk" when he stood up from a prone position.

One of the two previous doctors to examine Angus diagnosed hip dysplasia based upon breed, age, physical examination, and an x-ray. He prescribed a non-steroidal drug for Angus, but Angus' owner noticed no change in the dog after a 2-week trial with the drug.

The medical history provided by his owner revealed recurrent staphylococcal pyoderm, a common bacterial skin infection in dogs, that was responsive to various antibiotics. His original veterinarian had mentioned the possibility of atopy, a skin allergy, as a cause of Angus' constant itching and recurring skin infections, but no testing was done to determine whether Angus actually had the condition. Angus was fed a "premium obesity prevention diet," but he did not lose weight while eating this diet.

No pain was noted upon manipulation of the limbs. Pelvic limb swaying, resembling a drunken swagger, was noted; but no neurological deficits were detected in either the front or rear limbs. Cranial nerve functioning was within normal limits, indicating no problems or diseases of the brain. He seemed to have mild non-painful swelling of both front feet; fever was not detected. There was no exposure to external parasites, according to the owner.

When I listened to Angus' chest I noticed no abnormal heart or lung sounds; pulses were strong and regular. Abdominal and lymph node examination appeared to be normal and the peripheral lymph nodes were not enlarged. Grade II periodontal disease was detected, based upon excessive tartar on his teeth.

A voided urine sample was normal. A review of Angus' pelvic x-rays showed that they were underexposed with a "froggy view" of the hip joints because the films were made without sedation, and the correct view—required to properly evaluate the hip joints—was not obtained. Despite the shortcoming in his evaluation, it was apparent that hip dysplasia and secondary osteoarthritis were not the cause of Angus' clinical signs. As is so typical with at least half the cases that come to me for complementary therapies for "arthritis," Angus actually had perfectly normal hips that did not require treatment.

So what was the causing Angus' problems? Based on his sudden onset of lethargy and swaggering gait, I ordered a CBC and biochemical blood profile. These tests revealed high cholesterol, anemia, and very low thyroid hormone levels. The diagnosis was easy to make: Angus suffered from thyroid disease, hypothyroidism, which caused all his clinical signs and abnormal blood results.

Angus did not need non-steroidal drugs or anything else to treat arthritis because he did not have arthritis. Instead, I prescribed thyroid supplements and a weight-loss diet. Angus experienced complete resolution of his clinical signs and a return to normal of his blood values. To date he is doing very well, walking normally, and is near his ideal weight. Additionally, because hypothyroidism can cause chronic skin infections, now that his thyroid disease is under control, Angus experiences fewer skin infections.

I continually stress that you should obtain a proper diagnosis before embarking on chronic therapy for your dog's lameness. Administering medication such as corticosteroids or non-steroidal medications for 7 to 14 days, wait to see whether your pet pet improves. This can be useful in helping to determine whether the pet experiences any relief from the cause of the lameness. However, in my opinion, continuing to administer medication for longer periods of time without establishing the correct cause of the problem borders on neglect if not outright malpractice

In the next chapter, I'll discuss what should happen during your veterinary visit to allow the doctor to accurately diagnose the cause of your dog's lameness. First, so you can see the importance of a proper diagnosis, I will present other conditions that could cause your dog to act lame.

OLD AGE

YOU WILL GAIN at least three important points through reading this book. The first is that your dog deserves a proper diagnosis before receiving any chronic therapy for "arthritis." The second point is that your dog should receive potentially harmful medications such as non-steroidals or corticosteroids on a long-term basis *only* after all other safer treatments have failed—and then *only* with frequent careful monitoring to allow early detection of side effects including intestinal ulcers, kidney disease, and liver disease. The final important lesson is this: *Old age is not a disease!*

> With rare exceptions, abnormal clinical signs in pets have little to do with aging but are rather symptoms of disease.

Far too many pets have owners (and, sadly, even doctors) who do not care for them properly because they are just "acting old." With rare exceptions, abnormal clinical signs in pets have little to do with aging but are rather symptoms of disease. A normal older pet does not vomit frequently, eat more (or less), drink more (or less), or show signs of forgetfulness or lameness. All of these are symptoms of conditions that require prompt diagnosis and proper treatment. So while the older pet certainly has a higher incidence of diseases, including arthritis, don't ignore your pet's limp because he is old. To do so is a disservice to him and deprives him of all that geriatric medicine can do for him during his golden years.

Old age is not a disease. When any pet acts differently than normal, regardless of its age, please seek immediate professional care.

TRAUMA

WHETHER OR NOT you've witnessed physical trauma to your dog, your dog's lameness may be due to some simple injury. It is important that any lameness that lasts more than a day or two be diagnosed and treated to ease your dog's pain and prevent complications.

Fractures and Dislocations

Fractures and dislocations are most often the result of trauma, although bone infections, nutritional diseases, and cancer can weaken the bone enough to cause fractures and resulting lameness. Trauma is usually readily recognized by the owner, making the diagnosis quite easy and unlikely to be confused with arthritis. However, some congenital disorders (described on pages 27–29) cause joint dislocations and result in lameness without trauma. A thorough orthopedic and evaluation, including an x-ray, will most often result in early diagnosis and successful treatment.

Soft Tissue Injuries

Trauma may also cause soft tissue injuries that are not always quite as easily diagnosed as fractures and dislocations. Common soft tissue injuries include rupture of the cruciate ligaments of the knee joints and tearing of the collateral ligaments of the knee joints, similar to the injury seen in people.

Suspect soft tissue injuries when your dog has a sudden onset of lameness following exercise, often an activity that involves sudden "starts and stops" or twisting of the knee joints.

When a soft tissue injury is the culprit, radiographs are usually normal, although the rare pet with subtle and undiagnosed chronic ligament injuries will, of course, have secondary arthritis. Under anesthesia, pets with ligamentous tears will show increased joint looseness when the affected joint is manipulated in comparison to the normal joint on the opposite leg. Some cases require definitive diagnosis during surgical or arthroscopic examination of the joint.

Some soft tissue injuries are minor, such as a bruise, muscle tear, or a thorn or glass in the paw. Usually these heal with rest and time. The only cure for more serious soft tissue injuries involves surgery. I believe recovery is enhanced when surgery is combined with complementary therapies such as glucosamine, PSGAG therapy, nutritional supplements, and oral fatty acids. Herbs, acupuncture, and other therapies can aid in healing and offer pain relief.

Neurological Disorders

Several neurological disorders cause dogs to show signs similar to arthritis.

Disk Disease

Disk disease generally causes paralysis, pain, or both rather than true lameness. Still, since the pain from a protruding disk can cause decreased mobility, it would not be uncommon to see a "slow-moving" pet that appears to be lame. Disk disease is most common in smaller breeds of dogs such as Dachshunds.

Just like your backbone, your dog's backbone, or spine, is made up of bones called vertebrae. In between the vertebrae are "shock-absorbing" disks made of cartilage. These disks protect the ends of the vertebrae and absorb the impact or shock that is transmitted to the spine as the pet moves, runs, jumps, and walks.

Disk disease occurs as the shock-absorbing disks degenerate. As de-generative changes arise, the elasticity of the disk is gone, calcification of the disk occurs, and the disk can no longer function as a shock absorber. With time, the center and sometimes outer part of the disk degenerates to the point where it actually protrudes into the spinal canal, placing pressure on spinal nerves or even the spinal cord itself. This pressure causes pain and even paralysis in severe cases, depending upon the location of the protrusion within the spinal canal and amount of disk protruding into the canal.

Many cases of disk disease respond well to acupuncture and nutritional supplements, the less severe cases responding the best.

Suspect disk disease if you have a smaller dog that shows signs of back pain or paralysis of the front or rear limbs. To identify disk disease, the dog is usually sedated and the spine x-rayed. Calcified disks, when they occur, are easily identified. However, in over half of the cases I see, a special procedure such as a myelogram, CT scan, or MRI scan is needed to locate the disk protrusion.

Treatment varies depending on the severity of the signs. Low doses of corticosteroids or non-steroidal drugs can be used to provide immediate relief from pain and relieve nerve swelling; cage rest is essential to allow healing. Surgery is recommended in severe cases that result in paralysis, or in cases of chronic pain and discomfort. Many cases of disk disease respond well to acupuncture and nutritional supplements, the less severe cases responding the best.

Wobbler's Syndrome

Wobbler's syndrome is an interesting cause of abnormal swaying movements of the hind limbs called ataxia. The typical gait seen in pets with ataxia resembles someone walking when drunk; the pet displays a swaying, wobbly movement or unsteadiness when trying to walk.

The condition is seen most often in larger breeds of dogs, especially 4- to 8-month-old Great Danes and 4-year-old and older Doberman Pinschers. The underlying cause is unknown, although genetics, joint defects, and excessive nutrition when young are all possibilities.

Dobermans and Great Danes that walk funny should be checked for Wobbler's Syndrome. Wobbler's Syndrome involves lesions (injuries) that include one or more of the following problems: malformed vertebrae in the neck, protruding intervertebral disk in the neck, thickening of the ligaments surrounding the vertebrae in the neck, and instability of the vertebrae in the neck area.

Diagnosis is based on clinical signs and radiographs. Your veterinarian will probably need to perform special studies such as a myelogram, CT scans, or MRI scans to accurately pinpoint the lesion. Mild cases can improve with corticosteroids, acupuncture, and nutritional supplements. More severe cases may require surgical correction.

Cauda Equina Syndrome

The lower back, or lumbosacral joint, is a common site of disease in dogs, specifically in the larger breeds. Cauda equina syndrome refers to any lesion, usually an intervertebral disk, that causes compression of the nerves in this area of the spine.

Suspect cauda equina syndrome if your dog seems to be in pain when she moves, is reluctant to jump, exhibits pain when her lower back is manipulated or stroked, or shows hind limb stiffness or lameness. Neurological signs such as dragging one or both rear limbs, paralysis, and urinary or fecal incontinence can also occur.

The diagnosis is made under sedation through x-ray and special tests such as myelography, CT scans, or MRI scans when needed. Conventional treatment utilizes steroids or non-steroidal medications to control pain and surgery in severe cases. Acupuncture and nutritional supplements can offer alternatives to conventional treatment.

Fibrocartilage Embolus

Fibrocartilage embolus (FCE for short) is a rare, ill-defined, and difficult-to-diagnose disorder most commonly affecting larger breeds of dogs. In this condition, an acute onset of paralysis results, usually occurring after exercise or exertion. Although the exact cause is unknown, FCE is thought to

CAUSES OF LAMENESS IN DOGS

Osteoarthritis

Old Age

Trauma
- Fractures and Dislocations
- Soft Tissue Injuries

Neurological Disorders
- Intervertebral Disk Disease
- Wobbler's Syndrome
- Cauda Equina Syndrome
- Fibrocartilage Embolus

Autoimmune Diseases
- Lupus
- Rheumatoid Arthritis
- Drug-Induced
- Vaccine-Induced
- Dermatomyositis
- Polymyositis and Polyarthritis
- Thyroid Disease

Cancer

Congenital Disorders
- Dysplasia
- Mucopolysacchraidosis

Infectious Arthritis
- Lyme Disease
- Hepatozoon

Other
- Overuse Syndrome
- Osteochondrosis
- Panosteitis
- Spondylosis Deformans
- Gout

occur because a microscopic piece of the fibrocartilaginous intervertebral disk somehow breaks away and travels as an embolus that then lodges in a blood vessel supplying the spinal cord. The paralysis usually affects only one side of the body, but this varies depending upon the location of the embolus.

Suspect FCE if your dog goes lame suddenly, especially right after exercise. Because no easy specific test is available for this condition, your veterinarian will make the diagnosis from the dog's medical history and negative findings for everything else on routine radiographs. Although there is no conventional treatment that is effective, most dogs will recover on their own with supportive care, if needed.

AUTOIMMUNE DISEASES

AN AUTOIMMUNE DISEASE is one in which the dog's body literally turns on itself. Basically, the pet's immune system can no longer recognize its own normal tissues but will treat its own tissues as if they are foreign invaders. The pet forms antibodies against its own cells, wreaking havoc and widespread destruction throughout the body. Lameness is a characteristic of several autoimmune diseases.

Lupus

Lupus is the common name for a disease called systemic lupus erythematosus, or SLE. This disease is among the most common in the category of autoimmune diseases. In pets and people with lupus, antibodies are formed against a variety of tissues including the joints, the skin, muscles, kidneys, and bone marrow (causing anemia, low white blood cell counts, and low platelet counts). Because so many tissues can be affected by lupus, resulting in a variety of clinical signs, the disease is often called the "great imitator." Signs can be vague, intermittent, and resemble many other conditions.

Because lupus resembles many other conditions and is very difficult to diagnose, it is easily overlooked as a cause of chronic lameness. While lupus is not a common cause of lameness in dogs, lameness is the most common sign of lupus in dogs, being present in approximately 75 percent of affected animals.

> An autoimmune disease is one in which the dog's body literally turns on itself.

Once other common causes of lameness have been ruled out, consider lupus as a possible culprit. Diagnosis is based upon clinical signs and often numerous laboratory tests since no one specific "lupus test" exists.

Conventional treatment involves high immunosuppressive doses of corticosteroids or other chemotherapeutic drugs. Complementary care includes supportive care through nutritional supplements.

Rheumatoid Arthritis

Rheumatoid arthritis is another uncommon autoimmune cause of lameness. In this condition, the dog's body forms antibodies against its own joints. This crippling disease causes typical signs of arthritis, including stiffness that is often pronounced in the morning, reluctance to exercise, pain upon manipulation of the joints, and swelling of the involved joints. Rheumatoid arthritis causes more discomfort than does osteoarthritis, which causes discomfort but is rarely very painful. Pets with rheumatoid arthritis may be so severely affected that they cannot walk.

Suspect rheumatoid arthritis if you notice joint swelling, severe pain, and morning stiffness. Diagnosis is based on laboratory testing including x-rays of the joint, negative joint tap for bacteria and other infectious organisms, and a positive rheumatoid arthritis RF (which stands for rheumatoid factor) blood test.

Rheumatoid arthritis is treated with analgesics (nonsteroidal medications for pain), corticosteroids, and other chemotherapeutic immunosuppressive medications. Or your veterinarian may try nutritional supplements that are useful for the control of osteoarthritis if your dog develops rheumatoid arthritis. Acupuncture that stimulates immune-enhancing points can be tried as well.

Drug-Induced

While still rare, many doctors feel that drug-induced joint problems are becoming more common. Your dog's immune system can react to any drug, and drugs are usually considered foreign substances. A hypersensitivity or allergic reaction occurs when antibodies form chemical complexes with the administered drug; these drug-antibody complexes are then deposited into the joints of the body. The drugs most commonly associated with drug-induced lameness are antibiotics, especially sulfa drugs, erythromycin, penicillins, and cephalosporins.

Suspect a drug-induced problem when signs appear and worsen while the pet is taking a medication and improvement is seen within 2 to 7 days of stopping the medication. Genetics may play a role in the development of this syndrome as well. Doberman Pinschers are predisposed to develop drug-induced lameness when administered sulfa drugs.

Since combinations of medications can cause acute lameness, it is important that you tell your veterinarian about all medicines, including heartworm and flea-prevention medicines, that you give to your pet.

Vaccine-Induced

One of the problems blamed on the ever-increasing use of vaccines is immune disorders, including immune arthritis. Vaccine-induced immune arthritis is occasionally seen following immunization, most often with distemper vaccination in puppies. The general feeling among veterinarians is that, in a very small number of pets, the distemper vaccine may be involved in some causes of immune arthritis, as distemper vaccine particles have been found in some of the affected joints.

> Suspect vaccine-induced immune arthritis if your dog shows signs of lameness soon after receiving a vaccination.

Suspect vaccine-induced immune arthritis if your dog shows signs of lameness soon after receiving a vaccination. The problem usually resolves on its own and does not seem to recur with adult immunizations. Immune arthritis is just one of a variety of problems that the unnecessary immunization of pets can cause.

The holistic approach to immunizations, which utilizes vaccine titers, will help decrease vaccine-related problems while still offering protection against infectious diseases.

Dermatomyositis

Dermatomyositis, a condition affecting mainly young Collies and Shetland Sheepdogs, is characterized by a skin condition and muscle inflammation. The cause is unknown, but the condition appears to be an autoimmune disease. Mildly affected dogs recover spontaneously but more seriously affected pets may require treatment with immunosuppressive medications.

Polymyositis and Polyarthritis

Polymyositis is an autoimmune disease where antibodies that attack the pet's muscle tissues are formed. Polyarthritisis a disease involving the formation of antibodies that attack the pet's joints. Both polymyositis and polyarthritis may occur in the same pet simultaneously.

Suspect polymyositis when you see stiffness and poor exercise tolerance. Muscle atrophy and pain may be present as well. Diagnosis is made through doing muscle biopsies, analyzing joint fluid, and ruling out other diseases. Conventional therapy is the same as that for other immune-related disorders; complementary therapies can be helpful to regulate the immune system and relieve pain.

Thyroid Disease

Hypothyroidism, or low thyroid disease, is probably the most common endocrine or hormonal disease in dogs. It is usually considered an autoimmune disease, where the dog's body forms antibodies against its own thyroid glands. These antibodies result in the thyroid gland producing too little of the thyroid hormone.

Thyroid disease is under-diagnosed and is often the cause of a whole host of chronic diseases in dogs.

When I was in school, we learned that the "classic signs" of hypothyroidism in dogs were obesity, hair loss, and the pet seeking warm places. Over the last few years, doctors have come to discover that thyroid disease can have clinical signs and resemble *any* number of diseases. Rarely do I see a pet with the "classic signs" of thyroid disease.

Angus, the Rottweiler I described at the beginning of this chapter, is a very unusual example of hypothyroidism.

While quite unusual, Angus demonstrates that another disorder can cause signs that resemble arthritis. Failing to respond to the appropriate dose of non-steroidal medication should prompt a search for another disorder, as just about every dog with arthritis quickly improves with nonsteroidal medication. Because a number of disorders can cause arthritis-like symptoms, proper diagnostic testing is imperative so that your veterinarian can make the correct diagnosis and offer the best treatment, as will be discussed in the next chapter.

CANCER

SEVERAL CANCERS AFFECT the bones in pets and the resulting lameness that can resemble arthritis. Most of these tumors are primary tumors arising from the bone, rather than metastatic tumors that have spread from other locations in the body. Each year an estimated 8,000 to 10,000 dogs will be diagnosed with bone cancer in the U.S.

The most common tumors affecting bones, joints, and surrounding soft tissues in dogs are osteosarcoma, chondrosarcoma, fibrosarcoma, liposarcoma, and histiocytosis, which is found in Bernese mountain dogs. Osteosarcoma, however, is the most common tumor affecting the bones of dogs, accounting for 85 to 90 percent of all bone tumors. Usually, middle-aged dogs of the larger breeds are affected. The bones most commonly diseased with osteosarcoma include the radius (forearm), humerus (upper arm), tibia (shin bone), and femur (upper leg bone).

If your pet has a swollen limb, have it examined immediately to check for bone cancer.

Diagnosis is made by radiographs and bone biopsy. If your veterinarian diagnoses your dog as having bone cancer, insist on a chest radiograph to detect the spread of the tumor before you submit your pet to a surgical procedure that would be unnecessary if the cancer has spread at the time of diagnosis.

With early diagnosis, bone cancer is not usually curable but is treatable with aggressive therapies. Conventional treatment requires surgical removal of the tumor, most commonly limb amputation, and chemotherapy. Some specialized facilities offer limb-sparing surgery in selected cases, which allows the dog to keep the limb after surgical removal of the tumor and affected bone. Complementary therapy includes a number of herbs and nutrients intended to stimulate the immune system of the pet in an attempt to increase longevity and improve the quality of life for the dog.

> Complementary therapy includes a number of herbs and nutrients intended to stimulate the immune system of the pet in an attempt to increase longevity and improve the quality of life for the dog.

CONGENITAL DISORDERS

CONGENITAL DISORDERS ARE those that are present at birth, and are usually considered inherited, although they may not actually show up for months or years. Purebred

CONGENITAL ORTHOPEDIC PROBLEMS OF DOGS

The following are some of the various orthopedic conditions diagnosed in dogs that may be confused with osteoarthritis. While any breed of dog could potentially be affected with any of these conditions, those breeds most commonly affected are listed.

Atlantoaxial Dislocation Chihuahua, Pekingese, Pomeranian, Poodle, Yorkshire Terrier

Cauda Equina German Shepherd

Elbow Dysplasia German Shepherd, Labrador Retriever, Basset Hound, French Bulldog, Great Dane, Bull Mastiff, Great Pyrenees, Irish Wolfhound, Weimaraner, Newfoundland

Hip Dysplasia Mainly any large or giant breed, also Cocker Spaniel and Shetland Sheepdog (Sheltie)

Mucopolysaccharidosis VI Miniature Pinscher

Osteoporosis Dachshund

Panosteitis German Shepherd, Basset Hound, and other breeds

Patellar (kneecap) Dislocation Toy breeds

Shoulder Dislocation Chihuahua, Griffon, King Charles Spaniel, Miniature Poodle, Miniature Pinscher, Pomeranian, Wirehaired Fox Terrier

Wobbler's Syndrome Basset Hound, Doberman Pinscher, English Sheepdog, Fox Terrier, Great Dane, Irish Setter, Rhodesian Ridgeback, Saint Bernard

dogs should be screened early in life for the presence of congenital problems that can cause disease later in life. Dogs that carry a congenital disorder should not be bred.

Several congenital disorders affecting the skeletal system can cause signs of lameness mimicking arthritis.

Dysplasia

Hip dysplasia can occur in any breed of dog, including the smaller breeds, but is most common in larger breeds such as Labrador and Golden Retrievers and German Shepherds. Shoulder dislocation is most common in smaller breeds such as the Chihuahua, Yorkshire Terrier, and Miniature Poodle. Elbow dislocations are also typically considered a large dog problem. Dislocations of the kneecap more commonly affect smaller breeds. Atlantoaxial dislocation is a condition in which the articulation between the skull and spine dislocates, usually affecting smaller breeds.

If not diagnosed properly when clinical signs are first seen, osteoarthritis can develop with time due to chronic strain on the dislocating joint, causing additional problems. Most of these conditions respond well to early surgical correction.

Mucopolysaccharidosis

A rare inherited disease in pets, mucopolysaccharidosis affects the glycosaminoglycans, one of the building blocks of cartilage, of the joints. Affected pets exhibit swollen, painful joints, and often other signs such as motor and visual deficits. Diagnosis involves special testing and there is no treatment.

INFECTIOUS ARTHRITIS

INFECTIOUS SEPTIC ARTHRITIS is very rare in pets and most commonly would occur as a complication of joint surgery. However, one cause of infectious arthritis in dogs, Lyme disease, is becoming more common in certain areas of the country.

Lyme Disease

A very specific type of infectious arthritis is Lyme disease, also called *Lyme borelliosis*. This condition is caused by a bacterium (specifically a spirochete) transmitted by the bite of a tick. The disease is not transmitted directly from pet to pet or between pets and their owners, as the organism must mature in the body of the tick and then be transmitted through the tick bite.

In people, a characteristic rash called erythema migrans is often located at the site of the tick bite. This rash is usually not detected in pets because of the animal's fur. The disease in people can cause disorders of the musculoskeletal system, nervous system, and even the heart. In dogs, the most common presentation is lameness. Many dogs have a fever and swollen lymph nodes. Rarely do dogs show the neurological or cardiac problems seen in people with the disease.

Lyme disease can affect both pets and their owners. Tick prevention, therefore, is extremely important.

Once again the clinical signs resemble typical osteo-arthritis unless fever or joint swelling occurs. Pets living in areas of high tick concentrations are most at risk. To allow early diagnosis, have your pet tested for Lyme disease and the two other common tick-borne diseases (ehrlichiosis and Rocky Mountain spotted fever) approximately 30 days after noticing a tick on the pet.

Diagnosis is achieved through clinical signs and a positive blood test. Dogs previously immunized against Lyme disease will show a positive blood test on the screening test commonly used for diagnosis; a second blood test can be used to find out whether the first positive test resulted from the prior vaccination or a true incidence of the disease.

Prevention through tick control is suggested. Immunization for Lyme disease is controversial among holistic veterinarians. Most doctors do not recommend it. I offer Lyme vaccine only to clients whose pets have a great deal of tick exposure, and to date have noticed minimal acute side effects from the vaccine. A discussion with your doctor is in order if your pet has known tick exposure.

Treatment of Lyme disease is usually rewarding and involves administration of appropriate antibiotics; acupuncture can be used to lessen joint pain.

Hepatozoonosis

Hepatozoonosis is another infectious disease caused by a small parasitic organism called a coccidian. While found throughout the world, the coccidian is most common along the U.S. Gulf Coast. Transmission occurs when the pet ingests the tick that carries the coccidian organism, unlike most tick-related diseases that result from the tick biting the pet.

Suspect hepatozoonosis if you have seen ticks on your pet in the past, you live along or have recently visited the U.S. Gulf Coast, and you detect intermittent signs of the disease. Although the signs will vary in infected dogs, typical signs for hepatozoonosis include fever, weight loss, stiffness, discharge from the eyes and nose, and pain localized to the rear legs or spine. Signs are seen periodically, and some dogs seem to recover for a period of time before symptoms return.

Diagnosis requires a high degree of suspicion for the disease, as the signs are vague and not specific to hepatozoonosis; for this reason, the disease is easily misdiagnosed. Radiographs are suggestive and can rule out simple osteoarthritis, although both conditions can exist together. Blood tests are also suggestive but making a definitive diagnosis requires seeing the coccidial organism on biopsy or in the blood.

No one medicine is perfect for hepatozoonosis; in fact, it may be difficult if not impossible to cure. Treatment involves antibiotics and non-steroidal medication for pain relief. Also consider complementary therapies to boost the immune system and relieve pain.

OVERUSE SYNDROME

OVERUSE SYNDROME is a condition caused by an owner pushing the pet beyond its limits. More a problem in people and in very active dogs, overuse syndrome occurs in joints subject to repetitive strain. These joints include the hips, knees, ankle, and wrist joints. The more wear and tear on a joint, the more likely the joint will suffer inflammation and damage. Simply resting the joint allows healing; a short course of a non-steroidal medication, acupuncture, or other complementary therapy can be used as well.

The case of Missy comes to mind when I think of overuse syndrome. Missy is a middle-aged Shetland Sheepdog (Sheltie) that has confirmed hip dysplasia and mild secondary osteoarthritis. Missy is doing quite well on nutritional supplements, including glucosamine, chondroitin, vitamin C, and omega-3 fatty acids.

The problem is not Missy so much as her owner, who loves to play hard with Missy. Her daily routine is to run Missy in the park for hours on end. The next day Missy is sore, reluctant to move, and often quite miserable. Within 2 to 3 days of rest, however, Missy is back to normal.

While dogs with osteoarthritis can and should exercise (see chapter 8), Missy's owner obviously pushes her much too hard. When this happens, Missy pays the price later. By minimizing the stress on Missy's hips through less strenuous exercise, Missy would not suffer following her day at the park. By educating Missy's owner and finding out just what level of exercise will not cause Missy to suffer, we can maximize her enjoyment as a pet without causing her undue suffering.

OSTEOCHONDROSIS

OSTEOCHONDROSIS IS A common cause of lameness in large breed puppies. Rapid growth, overexertion, and excessive use of calcium supplements have been linked to osteochondrosis.

Osteochondrosis refers to a condition of unknown origin characterized by abnormal cartilage development in a young, growing dog. In pets with osteochondrosis, the growing cartilage fails to develop normally. Thickening of the joint cartilage occurs, with microscopic fissures and fractures subsequently developing. With normal stresses placed on the abnormal cartilage as the puppy runs and plays, a tiny flap of cartilage can separate from the remaining joint cartilage that covers the ends of the bones that comprise the joint. The flap may calcify with time; this is easy to see when the joint is radiographed.

The exact reason why some puppies develop osteochondrosis is not known. Several theories have been proposed to explain the possible cause, including some relating to genetics, trauma, and nutrition. Trauma is mainly a disease of large, rapidly growing breeds of puppies who tend to be quite rambunctious (as owners of these breeds readily attest!). Nutrition may trigger the condition, as many of these puppies have been overfed to produce extremely rapid growth, and many have also received excessive calcium in their diets.

Vitamin C deficiency has been shown to cause osteochondrosis among other problems, although this is unlikely to occur in dogs because they, unlike people, manufacture their own vitamin C. Still, many holistic doctors feel that giving additional vitamin C to growing puppies can prevent the occurrence of osteochondrosis and other problems such as hip dysplasia, while conventional veterinarians refute these claims. As a potential "preventive" measure in puppies, one holistic veterinarian recommends giving vitamin C to pregnant female dogs and to the newborn puppies after whelping. He also uses vitamin C in his patients with osteoarthritis and osteochondrosis in an effort to encourage healing of the cartilage. Since the exact amount of vitamin C needed is unknown, the doctor recommends slowly increasing the amount given until mild diarrhea occurs (what is known as the bowel tolerance level), then reducing the dose slightly until the diarrhea disappears. This dose at which the diarrhea disappears becomes the therapeutic dose to use for that pet.

> Osteochondrosis refers to a condition of unknown origin characterized by abnormal cartilage development in a young, growing dog.

The most common joints affected with osteochondrosis include the shoulder joint (the most common joint affected, and many puppies have both joints affected even if they are only lame on one leg at the time of initial diagnosis), elbow joint (often difficult to diagnose without special radiographic testing such as an MRI), knee joint, and ankle joint.

Suspect osteochondrosis if your dog suffers acute lameness initiated by a recent mild traumatic event, such as catching a ball. The lameness may resolve on its own or with the use of non-steroidal medication but will shortly return. Physical examination may show mild pain when the joint is manipulated. Due to the high incidence of osteochondrosis in rapidly growing larger breed puppies, this condition must remain uppermost on our list of possible diagnoses when a lame puppy is examined.

Radiographs of both the affected and unaffected joints are recommended since many puppies have both legs affected at the same time even though only one limb might be lame. Often special radiographs or surgical exploration of the joint is needed to allow proper diagnosis, especially in early cases when joint problems do not show on the radiographs.

Treatment involves surgically removing the damaged cartilage and any joint flaps that are seen in the joint. Your dog will benefit greatly through the preoperative and postoperative use of nutritional supplements designed to aid in cartilage repair, pain relief, and inflammation relief such as glucosamines, PSGAGS, and chondroitin. Animals with osteochondrosis should not be bred as the disease may be inherited.

PANOSTEITIS

PANOSTEITIS REFERS TO a condition causing lameness in the limbs of young larger breeds of dogs, especially the German Shepherd. Lameness typically lasts 1 to 2 months then resolves on its own, often to return in the same limb or another limb. The cause is unknown but suspected to be a result of genetics, metabolic diseases, blood vessel problems, or allergy.

Panosteitis is a condition that comes and goes and is often difficult to diagnose in its earliest stages.

In panosteitis, new bone grows in the marrow cavity of the bones of the limbs, causing pain, lameness, and sometimes fever. Radiographs will eventually reveal the diagnosis; radiographs may be normal if taken at the first signs of pain, but follow-up films taken a few weeks later usually reveal the problem.

The disease goes away after several months. However, affected puppies are uncomfortable and medications can be used to control pain. Nutritional supplements and acupuncture may also be helpful.

SPONDYLOSIS DEFORMANS

CALLED ANKYLOSING SPONDYLITIS in people, spondylosis deformans, or spondylosis for short, is an extremely common finding in older dogs of any breed. In this condition, extra bone grows below the spine in response to chronic wear and tear. This condition is basically considered arthritis of the spine. Even when spondylosis is found, it may or may not cause lameness.

Suspect spondylosis if your older dog is stiff when getting up or lying down, and does not want to jump. Diagnosis is easily made with spinal radiographs and by ruling out other causes of lameness. Most pets require no specific treatment, and certainly not drugs, unless they show clinical signs. For asymptomatic pets, complementary treatments include nutritional supplements such as glucosamine and chondroitin and omega-3 fatty acids to provide nourishment for the cartilage. Acupuncture can be used as needed for dogs in pain.

GOUT

GOUT, WHILE SOMEWHAT common in people, is extremely rare in pets. It is caused by sodium urate crystals forming in the joints. Diagnosis is made by radiographs of the joints and aspiration of the joints. The substance taken from the joints is examined microscopically to check for the crystals. Conventional therapy relies on anti-gout medication and changing the dog's diet to decrease the chances of urate crystal formation.

MISCELLANEOUS CAUSES OF LAMENESS

A NUMBER OF rare peculiarities can manifest in varying degrees of lameness. For example, Doberman Pinschers can be afflicted with a condition called dancing Doberman disease. Affected dogs hold up one rear limb while standing, often alternating with the opposite rear limb in a dancing motion. The cause is unknown but genetics is suspected; there is no treatment. This and other rare and peculiar problems are only diagnosed with a knowledge of breed-specific problems after ruling out just about every other possible problem.

Now that you've seen the number of conditions that can mimic osteoarthritis and understand why establishing a proper diagnosis early in the course of the disease is so critical, let's talk about what to expect during your visit with your pet's doctor.

CHAPTER SUMMARY

• Osteoarthritis is the most common cause of lameness in dogs but not the only cause.

• The true cause of your dog's lameness must be diagnosed professionally.

• Old age is not a reason to ignore your dog's lameness.

• Consider other causes if your dog's signs do not match those of osteoarthritis.

• Look for other causes if your dog's signs do not go away after taking arthritis medication for one week.

• Some, but not all, causes of lameness in dogs are breed specific.

·3·

What Can I Expect at My Veterinary Visit?

THE KIND OF CARE a veterinarian will give a dog showing signs of lameness depends upon the doctor. A "100 percent conventional" doctor whose mind is closed to complementary therapies will have one approach, while a "100 percent complementary" doctor whose mind is closed to conventional therapies will offer a totally different treatment. The doctor who is "100 percent conventional" won't be open to using therapies such as acupuncture, herbal medicine, and nutritional supplements. Instead, he or she will prefer to use unlimited medications and often recommend surgery. Some of these doctors will also offer little in the way of diagnostics, preferring instead to try various medications and take a "wait and see" approach.

Conversely, the doctor who is "100 percent complementary" will probably not be open to using approved medications for short-term pain and inflammation relief, and may be totally opposed to any form of surgery. These doctors too may use relatively little conventional diagnostic testing, instead preferring to treat your pet based upon clinical signs or "alternative" diagnostic techniques such as reflex testing.

I believe the best doctors are those who are truly holistic, who offer both conventional and complementary therapy options, as I present in this book. By being open-minded yourself, willing to doing whatever is in your pet's best interest, you offer it the best care possible.

My encounter with Jet illustrates the importance of a good diagnosis. Jet, an 8-year-old male Rottweiler, was referred to me for acupuncture. He had exhibited lameness and the typical swaying gait of a larger breed dog afflicted with hip dysplasia. His previous doctor had taken radiographs under sedation that verified the suspicion of hip dysplasia with secondary arthritis. My examination confirmed this diagnosis. Since Jet's owner did not want to use medications to control his signs if at all possible, I was contacted about using acupuncture on Jet.

I prescribed a regimen of twice weekly acupuncture treatments in addition to nutritional supplements containing glucosamine, chondroitin, and vitamin C. After several treatments, Jet was obviously not improving and was in fact worsening. He developed a low-grade fever, decreased appetite, increased joint stiffness, and swelling around the joints. Jet's failure to respond to treatment indicated a need to reassess our initial diagnosis. While his referring doctor and I both knew Jet had hip dysplasia compounded by osteoarthritis, his new clinical signs indicated something else was going on with Jet as well. I referred him to a specialist who performed further testing that indicated Jet had lupus. He responded well to medication to control the disease. Since his owner preferred not to travel to our office for continuing acupuncture therapy, we continued with supplements for his osteoarthritis to decrease his lameness.

PRACTICING HOLISTIC MEDICINE

AS I PRESENT lectures to pet owners and give interviews to promote this series of health guides, I'm often asked why more doctors don't practice holistic medicine. There are, I believe, several answers to this question.

First, veterinarians aren't specifically trained to be holistic doctors. Few, if any, veterinary schools teach about wellness programs and disease prevention. As of this writing, only five even offer courses in holistic medicine. We are just now beginning to see a focus on wellness and holistic care in medical schools; veterinary schools, I believe, will eventually adapt to this philosophy as well, but it will take some time.

Traditional pharmacology courses taught at school focus only on traditional drug therapies and ignore the more natural treatments such as herbal remedies. While learning about the many wonderful medications available is vitally important to the veterinarian-in-training, hearing a few lectures on more natural treatments would help expose the doctors-to-be to these exciting therapies.

When I was in school, the focus was on diagnosis and treatment of diseases through recognition of signs and symptoms. While it certainly is important to diagnose and treat diseases, I believe it's more important to prevent as many of these problems as possible.

The second reason few doctors practice holistic medicine is that it takes time, and a lot of it. Standard veterinary practices book four or more appointments per hour, thanks to a well-trained, fully leveraged staff. Because it takes longer to develop a complete patient history and personalize a wellness/disease prevention program for each patient, the holistic practice books just one to two appointments per hour.

The third reason that few veterinarians practice holistic medicine is fear. A large number of doctors still believe that anything other than conventional medicine is "quackish." I receive a lot of mail from doctors who are upset that I propose treatments that have not been subjected to a number of double-blind studies. While I too hope for the day when more complementary therapies will receive funding to undergo these rigorous trials, I must accept the clinical data we now have and do what I know can help my patients. True, there are certainly some charlatans out there, and some complementary treatments of questionable value, but by and large considerable evidence attests to the success of most mainstream complementary therapies. I don't think I need to run expensive clinical studies to show, for example, that the 10,000-year-old practice of acupuncture has merit. This is one therapy that has stood the test of time. The use of glucosamine products, while scoffed at when first suggested 10 to 15 years ago, is now accepted practice for treating osteoarthritis, as you will learn in this book.

Finding a Holistic Veterinarian

You may have to do some research to find a really good doctor who has this much-needed holistic philosophy. Begin by evaluating your pet's current veterinarian. If he or she is open to complementary therapies, your current doctor can treat your pet's basic needs with a holistic approach, referring you to a doctor who performs complementary therapies when those are indicated. If your doctor is not a holistic doctor, find one who is.

Note: As an aside, most doctors—even those who do not offer services like acupuncture and herbal medicine—

are using nutritional supplements such as glucosamine, shark cartilage, and perna mussels as part of their therapy for arthritic pets. This means your own doctor might be able to offer your arthritic pet some basic complementary therapy without your needing a referral. My hope is that the trend toward using supplements as part of the treatment of various diseases will continue.

If your dog does not have a current doctor, or has seen a doctor you do not feel will treat your pet holistically, ask someone who uses a holistic veterinarian for a referral. In addition to asking dog-owning friends, try asking for a referral at the local health-food store, pet store, or natural grocery store. Such stores often have directories with advertisements of holistic doctors and holistic veterinarians as they frequently get requests for referrals. You might also consult your phone book for veterinarians advertising holistic care.

> If he or she is open to complementary therapies, your current doctor can treat your pet's basic needs with a holistic approach, referring you to a doctor who performs complementary therapies when those are indicated.

If he or she is open to complementary therapies, your current doctor can treat your pet's basic needs with a holistic approach, referring you to a doctor who performs complementary therapies when those are indicated.

Finally, contact the American Holistic Veterinary Medical Association. You can reach this organization at 410-569-0795 and ask for referrals to holistic veterinarians in your area.

ASK THE VETERINARIAN

Whether in person or on the telephone, you want to interview the prospective holistic doctor who might end up treating your dog. After explaining that your dog is experiencing lameness and your desire to participate in a holistic treatment program, ask the veterinarian these basic questions and listen carefully for appropriate answers.

ASK: *How do you make a definitive diagnosis of osteoarthritis?*
IDEAL ANSWER: Under heavy sedation or light anesthesia with a full orthopedic examination and radiographs.

ASK: *What are your feelings about using drugs to control pain?*
IDEAL ANSWER: Short-term use of corticosteroids or non-steroidal drugs is acceptable on an as-needed basis, and varies from case to case. Chronic use of these medications is limited to the very rare pet that does not respond to any other therapy. Also, regular (every 2 to 3 months) close monitoring of vital signs and laboratory testing are essential to allow early detection of serious and potentially fatal side effects, such as liver disease, kidney disease, or diabetes.

ASK: *What type of diet should my pet eat?*
IDEAL ANSWER: The most natural prepared food or homemade diet possible.

ASK: *How do you treat chronic cases of osteoarthritis?*
IDEAL ANSWER: Supplements, herbs, homeopathy, acupuncture, and conventional prescribed medications on a short-term, as-needed basis.

No method of tracking down a holistic doctor is fool-proof; use the methods presented here as a starting point. Compile a list of as many names as possible from these sources, then make an appointment to visit with each doctor on your list. Because your relationship with your pet's doctor is key to your pet's health, select a doctor with whom you get along. Make sure the doctor is open-minded to a variety of conventional and complementary therapies, and places your pet's health first.

What to Bring with You

In order to get the most from your holistic veterinary visit, you must be an active participant. Begin your participation before your dog's appointment, by gathering the following:

• Verify the onset of your dog's lameness. Be prepared with an accurate estimate of how long your pet has been troubled. If the problem occurs only occasionally, keep notes about the circumstances, such as after exercise or only in the morning, when the lameness happens.

• Provide all your dog's medical records or at least the name, address, and telephone numbers of all doctors your dog has visited. If you are visiting this doctor for a second opinion on a diagnosis, bring the results of any tests that have already been performed, and radiographs, if possible.

• Make notes of all treatments you have tried, both conventional and complementary, and any effect these treatments have had on your dog.

• Be sure to make the doctor aware of any medications, including heartworm medications and over-the-counter flea and tick preventions, that your dog is taking. Always bring in any medicine containers, even if empty, so the doctor can assess the prescription. Many times I find that the wrong dosage or dosing interval was prescribed, and this may account for the pet failing to improve.

• Know the ingredients and amounts of all food your dog eats.

• Track as much as possible your dog's bowel and urinary output and any other signs of your dog's general health.

THE DOCTOR VISIT

ONCE YOU'VE FOUND the perfect doctor for your pet and have arrived for your appointment, understanding what should happen during your visit is important. If this is your first visit, expect to spend anywhere from 30 to 60 minutes or more for the initial evaluation and diagnostic testing. The visit is divided into three parts: the medical history, examination, and laboratory evaluation.

The Medical History

The history you provide is vital in helping your veterinarian properly assess your pet. It serves as a guide in deciding to which areas of the body he or she should pay particular attention during the examination, and with selecting only those laboratory tests needed to arrive at a proper diagnosis. It is not uncommon for clients to bring me pages of notes they have made at home, as well as notes and medical records from a prior doctor, to aid in my search for the correct diagnosis and treatment.

Here are some typical questions your doctor may ask you about your pet:

1. What is your pet's diet?
2. Is your pet current on his preventive care (such as vaccinations when necessary, parasite control programs including heartworm medications if needed) and dental cleanings?
3. Are you concerned about any other problems in addition to the lameness? (Other problems may indicate a diagnosis other than osteoarthritis in the lame pet or indicate additional medical problems in your pet, both of which are common.)
4. If you've been to another doctor:
   What was the diagnosis?
   How was the diagnosis made?
   What treatment was prescribed?
   Was the treatment effective?
5. If you've done any home treatments:
   What treatments did you try?
   Did they help?

The Examination

After asking these and any other questions of importance, your doctor will commence with the physical examination. I like to break the physical down into three parts: general physical, orthopedic examination, and neurological examination.

The general physical allows the doctor to properly examine the pet from head to toe. During this part a good doctor offering holistic care will initially ignore the primary complaint of lameness and offer a full physical examination in order to detect any other problems that might exist. Sometimes these other problems relate to the lameness; other times they just exist coincidentally with the lameness. For example, suppose that during the overall physical the doctor discovers that the dog, originally brought in for lameness, has a heart murmur indicating heart disease, or a tumor on the body that might be cancer. These problems can't be ignored and might actually take priority over the original problem.

The orthopedic examination involves evaluating the musculoskeletal system. During this part of the examination the doctor should observe the pet at rest for general body condition, limb position, swelling of the limbs, and pain when the limbs are touched or manipulated. During limb manipulations the doctor will listen and feel for crepitation, which is a grating sensation that may indicate osteoarthritis. He or she will look to see if any joints have abnormal movements, which could indicate ligament injury, and watch the dog get up from a down position, walk, turn, and lay back down, looking for any signs of stiffness, pain, or reluctance to do any specific maneuver.

The final part of the examination is the neurological examination, particularly as it relates to the affected limbs. The doctor will be wondering: Is paralysis present? Are limb reflexes normal? Can the animal return a foot positioned in an unusual posture back to its normal position? Since over half of the dogs I see for evaluation of hip dysplasia actually have neurological disease rather than dysplasia and secondary arthritis, this part of the exam, which is often overlooked by many doctors, is critical.

The Laboratory Evaluation

The laboratory evaluation is often critical in helping determine the cause of your pet's lameness. It allows your veterinarian to distinguish subtle clues that he or she detected during the physical examination. Yet the laboratory evaluation is often the most neglected part of the evaluation of the lame animal. This is evident through the number of first-time visitors to my practice that have been treated for arthritis by other doctors with potentially harmful medications yet never had so much as a simple radiograph or blood test to even determine the correct diagnosis and treatment. Laboratory evaluations include diagnostic imaging, blood tests, and sometimes surgery.

Diagnostic Imaging

Medical pictures of your pet often reveal the cause of your dog's lameness. Just as with people, these tests are performed using machines, sometimes in the vet's office and sometimes in a separate laboratory. Common images are radiographs, MRI, CT scans, and myelograms.

The most basic diagnostic imaging test is conventional radiography (commonly called x-rays). This two-dimensional picture, using x-ray irradiation, allows the doctor to evaluate the dog's skeletal system. When performed correctly, most pets will not need other imaging tests to properly diagnose the cause of their lameness.

Modern x-ray machines are very safe and are calibrated to deliver only the tiny amount of x-ray energy needed to produce high-quality pictures. Most often two views are taken to allow the doctor to assess the involved area from perpendicular sides: a front-to-back view and a side-to-side view.

In some states, anesthesia is required as it is against the law for medical personnel to be in the room when radiographs are being taken.

Because even the best-trained pet will not lie still while his joints are placed in odd positions, most pets need to be

A CLOSER LOOK

MRI scans make use of powerful magnets to detect magnetic fields in the body; a computer then analyzes these magnetic fields and turns them into a picture. This test is especially useful in looking at soft tissues such as disks and ligaments that are not revealed on conventional radiographs. CT scans, formerly called CAT scans, use x-ray energy to produce a more detailed picture than that produced by regular radiographs. Myelograms involve injecting a dye into the body, normally the spinal canal, and then using conventional x-rays to show the dye. This test is used for pets suspected of having disk disease or spinal tumors. Any blockage or deviation of the dye column indicates the presence of a spinal lesion, allowing the surgeon to pinpoint where to make his incision. The dye used in a myelogram can on rare occasions produce side effects such as chemical meningitis or short-term seizures as the pet awakens from anesthesia. While these side effects are very rare with today's safer dyes, you should discuss any concerns you have about this procedure with your pet's doctor.

sedated to allow proper positioning and minimize the need for multiple radiograph exposures. In some states, anesthesia is required as it is against the law for medical personnel to be in the room when radiographs are being taken. Modern sedatives are safe when used properly and the pet is monitored carefully. In my practice the sedative is reversed at the completion of the radiograph procedure and the pet is fully awake within minutes.

Occasionally a conventional radiograph fails to reveal any abnormalities, and the doctor may order a more specialized test such as an MRI, CT scan, myelogram, or a bone scan. Again, the dog must be sedated to avoid movement during these tests.

Bone Scan

While not used as commonly in pets as in people, a bone scan might be needed if other tests fail to detect the cause of the pet's lameness and the doctor suspects any lesions that may be present in the bones. In this procedure, which must also be done under full anesthesia, a radioactive isotope is injected into the blood. Then, a special scanning camera is used to detect accumulations of the isotope at various points in the body, such as any areas

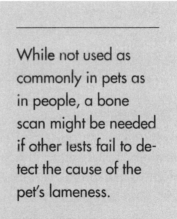

> While not used as commonly in pets as in people, a bone scan might be needed if other tests fail to detect the cause of the pet's lameness.

of bone that show inflammation, infection, or tumors. A computer assembles information from the camera and produces a picture for evaluation.

Blood Tests

Your veterinarian will often use blood count and blood profile to help diagnose diseases that might be the cause of your dog's lameness. The blood tests provide information on the general health of the pet, the presence of another existing disease, and your dog's tolerance for medication. For example, a blood test might reveal diabetes. While diabetes does not typically cause lameness, early detection of this hormonal problem will extend your pet's life by allowing treatment to begin before clinical disease is present.

> While diabetes does not typically cause lameness, early detection of this hormonal problem will extend your pet's life by allowing treatment to begin before clinical disease is present.

Blood tests also allow the doctor to determine whether he or she needs to alter the prescribed medications. The blood profile is important if medications (especially corticosteroids or non-steroidal medications) will be used for any length of time. Since non-steroidal medications, which many doctors typically prescribe for pets with osteoarthritis, can cause intestinal ulcers, kidney disease, and liver disease, determining whether your pet has any of these problems is important. If problems are present, the doctor may decide to lower the dose of the prescribed medication or even use a different medicine. And since non-steroidal drugs can actually cause these problems, the very few pets that must use these products on a long-term basis need to have blood tests at least every 2 to 3 months to allow early detection of potentially fatal complications from medical therapy.

External parasites such as ticks may or may not be a problem, depending on where you live. Ticks can carry diseases, including hepatozoonosis, ehrlichiosis, Rocky Mountain spotted fever, and Lyme disease—all of which can be transmitted to you. When indicated, your doctor may order additional blood tests to help determine whether a disease transmitted by a tick bite is the cause of your pet's lameness. Dogs previously vaccinated for Lyme disease will usually have a positive serological screening test. An additional test will be necessary to determine whether the positive result on the first test is due to vaccination or actual disease.

I routinely test pets with known tick exposure one month following detection of the ticks by the owner—even if the dog is not showing any clinical signs. Once again, early detection of these potentially fatal diseases will allow us to treat the pet before any problems develop.

When your pet's doctor suspects an immune cause of your pet's lameness, such as lupus or rheumatoid arthritis, he or she may order these special blood tests as well.

Fluid Analysis

Another common test that may be performed for diagnosing lameness in dogs is a synovial (joint) fluid analysis.

Whenever joint swelling is noticed, the doctor may insert a tiny needle into the joint and aspirate a small amount of fluid for analysis. The fluid is examined for the presence of inflammatory cells, bacteria, fungi, tumor cells, or immune cells to aid in diagnosis.

SURGERY

OCCASIONALLY ALL LABORATORY tests fail to reveal a diagnosis and your veterinarian will recommend surgery. If you are on a limited budget and cannot afford to have every possible test done, surgery may be a more affordable option for you. Arthroscopy and arthrotomy are the two common types.

In surgery, the doctor examines the affected joint in an effort to diagnose and treat the problem. This is most often the case where ligaments of the joint are torn, as is often the case with cruciate ligament injury of the knee joint. Arthroscopy uses a tiny instrument called an arthroscope to examine the joint, whereas arthrotomy utilizes a conventional surgical incision to open the joint. When practical, arthroscopy is preferred as the incision is smaller, side effects are less, and postoperative recovery time is decreased.

> If you are on a limited budget and cannot afford to have every possible test done, surgery may be a more affordable option for you.

Once your doctor has verified the presence of osteoarthritis through the medical history, physical examination, and any necessary laboratory test or surgery, he or she will review the various treatment options with you. The next chapter discusses the most commonly used conventional therapies, followed by a chapter presenting various complementary therapies that your doctor may prescribe for your arthritic dog.

CHAPTER SUMMARY

- To receive holistic care for your pet, you must seek out and consult a holistic veterinarian.

- You and the holistic veterinarian will work together to create the best treatment for your pet.

- Before your appointment, observe your dog carefully so that you can describe all signs and symptoms.

- Bring your dog's complete medical history and records of previous diagnosis to your appointment.

- In the office, the doctor will perform medical, orthopedic, and neurological examinations.

- The doctor will run a series of laboratory tests and perhaps surgery to provide a proper diagnosis.

· 4 ·

Conventional
Treatments for Arthritis

BEFORE DISCUSSING CONVENTIONAL treatments in this chapter, and complementary therapies in the next, I would like you to share with you what I believe is the "perfect" criteria in choosing a treatment approach for the dog with osteoarthritis:

1. The therapy should be cost-effective.
2. The therapy should be easy for the owner to administer.
3. The therapy must be safe for the pet.
4. The therapy must have minimal or no short- and long-term side effects.
5. The therapy should help the joint heal itself, as well as relieve inflammation and pain.

No matter what approach is ultimately chosen, it should meet as many of these conditions as possible to be of most benefit to the pet. As you will soon see, complementary therapies fill most of these requirements, whereas conventional medications do not and are rarely suitable as long-term therapy for most arthritic dogs. No type of treatment, conventional or complementary, should be administered on a long-term basis without a proper diagnosis.

Scooby is a classic example of failing to diagnose the disease and administering an incorrect treatment. Scooby is an 8-year-old Collie whose previous doctor had prescribed the new non-steroidal anti-inflammatory medication carprofen, known by the brand-name Rimadyl, for Scooby's presumed arthritis several months ago. Rimadyl can be a wonderful drug when used correctly. However, over 50 percent of the pets I evaluate have conditions for which Rimadyl should never have been prescribed. This was the case with Scooby, as he unfortunately was not improving. His owner saw no change in Scooby's gait and felt it was still painful for Scooby to get up from a seated position. I asked Scooby's owner what type of diagnostic testing was done to confirm the idea that Scooby really had osteoarthritis. According to the owner, no testing was done on Scooby. Based upon his large breed and middle-to-geriatric age Scooby's previous doctor had guessed that Scooby suffered from osteoarthritis.

> No type of treatment, conventional or complementary, should be administered on a long-term basis without a proper diagnosis.

I suspected that Scooby was not in fact arthritic. Just about every dog with osteoarthritis quickly responds to Rimadyl and similar medications, yet Scooby had not improved at all and had in fact worsened. I was also concerned about side effects from the drug, and asked Scooby's owner if any regular blood testing was done to check for ulcers or liver or kidney disease. Scooby's owner was surprised to hear there were side effects from the drug, and had been told how safe Rimadyl is when prescribed for osteoarthritis.

My examination and tests gave us the correct diagnosis. Scooby was not in fact arthritic but suffered from a condition called degenerative myelopathy, a degeneration of his spinal nerves. Unfortunately we don't have any very effective treatments for this progressive disorder, but we were able to stop administering Rimadyl and put Scooby on some nutritional supplements that can help some pets with his condition. The moral of Scooby's story is clear: get the proper diagnosis first, then use the correct treatment. Treating pets without the benefit of a correct diagnosis costs the owner unnecessary expenses and prolongs the problem for the pet. A few simple tests would have provided the correct diagnosis for Scooby much earlier. Fortunately, no long-term side effects from his non-steroidal treatment occurred.

How Conventional Therapies Work

CONVENTIONAL THERAPY FOR pets with osteoarthritis involves corticosteroids or non-steroidal medications and surgery. Unfortunately, some of these treatments do more to relieve the effects of the arthritis than to actually help the pet heal.

Remember that osteoarthritis is a painful condition of the joints. The pain pets with arthritis feel results from damaged cell membranes releasing chemicals that cause inflammation. At a minimum, the treatment selected must relieve the inflammation and pain, and for the long term, should encourage healing.

Various drugs work at different stages to help decrease the production of the chemicals that cause inflammation. For example, corticosteroids work at two places in this biochemical pathway: they help inhibit the enzyme responsible for metabolizing the membrane phospholipids into arachidonic and eicosapentaenoic acids, and they inhibit the enzyme responsible for breaking down arachidonic acid into pro-inflammatory compounds. Non-steroidal anti-inflammatory medications such as aspirin and ibuprofen work at another step in the pathway (called the COX pathway) that is responsible for metabolizing arachidonic acid into pro-inflammatory compounds.

> Many pets taking corticosteroids for prolonged periods of time gain weight as a side effect of this class of medication and this excess weight puts further stress on already damaged joints, adding more insult to injury.

Sadly, some conventional treatments are actually harmful to the joint cartilage. For example, many doctors choose long-term therapy with corticosteroids or non-steroidal medications for pets with osteoarthritis. While these drugs stop the pain the dog feels and decrease inflammations, most actually inhibit healing of the cartilage, further destroying the cartilage and joint components. So even though the pets will feel better for a while, we're actually making their condition worse. Many pets taking corticosteroids for prolonged periods of time gain weight as a side effect of this class of medication and this excess weight puts further stress on already damaged joints, adding more insult to injury.

CORTICOSTEROIDS

CORTICOSTEROIDS, OR STEROIDS for short, are the first class of medications that comes to mind when thinking of treating the arthritic dog. Steroids are also one of the most frequently used and abused drugs in veterinary and probably human medicine. It's just too easy for doctors to reach for the magic "steroid shot" to treat symptoms without really diagnosing and treating the disease. As a result, pets are often incorrectly treated for months or years before someone says "Enough. There must be a better way!"

Many of my holistic clients think that corticosteroids are horrible drugs to be avoided at all costs. However, that is far from the truth. Corticosteroids are actually wonderful drugs that can be life-saving when used correctly at the right dosage, for the proper length of time, and in a patient whose diagnosis suggests a disease most correctly treated with corticosteroids. The problem is that these drugs are often not used at the right dose, for the proper length of time, and in the right patient. Because they can aggravate existing osteoarthritis by inhibiting the synthesis of proteoglycans and collagen (the molecules that make up cartilage), there is rarely if ever a need for their long-term use in the treatment of most patients with arthritis.

What Steroids Do

As I mentioned, corticosteroids do a number of wonderful things. First, they are anti-inflammatory and analgesic pain-relieving medications. They decrease inflammation and swelling, relieving pain caused by inflammation, and relieve itching. Their ability to relieve itching leads many doctors to also over-prescribe them for pets with allergic dermatitis.

A CLOSER LOOK

So just what are corticosteroids? Why do so many in the health-care field seem so eager to use these miracle drugs? Cortico-steroids, or more correctly glucocorticoids, are hormones pro-duced by the adrenal glands under the control of the pituitary gland. When the body needs to produce more of its own gluco-corticoids, the pituitary gland produces a hormone called adrenocorticotrophic hormone (ACTH) that stimulates the adrenal gland to produce more glucocorticoids. When the level of gluco-corticoids rises, the pituitary shuts off its ACTH signal to the adre-nal gland; when the level of glucocorticoids falls, the pituitary puts out more ACTH. This loop keeps the body's production of glucocorticoids in check with the body's demand. However, if we give the pet corticosteroids as a treatment the pituitary gland senses this and stops production of ACTH so the adrenal glands won't make any more steroid. This effectively shuts down the body's normal production of a vitally important hormone. This won't hurt the pet if we use a low dose of steroid for a short pe-riod of time such as 7 to 10 days. However, if we use more potent steroids for longer periods of time and then suddenly stop giving the pet steroids, its body can't quickly adapt to the need for steroid and serious problems may result. This is one of the poten-tially serious side effects that occurs when we treat pets with glucocorticoids.

They are also very helpful in the initial treatment of patients with severe shock and neurological disease, such as relieving the inflammation after spinal cord and brain injuries.

Side Effects of Steroids

The negative side of these wonderful effects is that steroids can decrease the ability of wounds to heal and increase the chance of infection if used for too long or at high doses. Pets that truly need long-term steroid therapy also need careful, frequent monitoring to allow for early detection of infections. Steroids may also contribute to further destruction of arthritic joints by decreasing collagen and proteoglycan synthesis, making them a poor choice of long-term therapy for most pets with arthritis. Corticosteroids are also immunosuppressive. At a high enough dose, steroids suppress the body's immune system. While this can be useful in combatting immune diseases where the body is attacking itself, an animal with a suppressed immune system is more prone to infections.

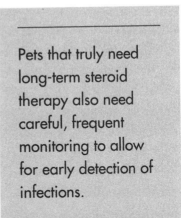

Pets that truly need long-term steroid therapy also need careful, frequent monitoring to allow for early detection of infections.

Commonly seen short-term side effects of corticosteroids that you should be concerned about include an increase in appetite, an increase in water intake, and an increase in urine output. These side effects are commonly observed in most if not all dogs undergoing corticosteroid therapy. Even those pets taking the medications for a short time and at a very low dose

LONG-TERM SIDE EFFECTS OF CORTICOSTEROID THERAPY IN DOGS

The long-term side effects of corticosteroid therapy on nearly every organ of a dog's body can do serious damage to your pet's quality of life. In addition, the use of steroids upsets laboratory tests, making artificial changes in liver enzymes, white blood cell values, and thyroid tests that may cause the misdiagnosis of other problems, such as these:

- Heart and cardiovascular system problems causing hypertension (high blood pressure) and sodium and water retention.
- Skin effects causing acne, infections, excessive bruising, atrophy (degeneration or thinning) of the skin, and hair loss.
- Hormonal problems, including infertility, growth failure, adrenal gland diseases, birth defects, and miscarriage.
- Gastrointestinal upset such as ulcers, pancreatitis, and perforation.
- Immune system suppression and decreased ability to resist infections.
- Metabolic problems such as increased blood fat, fatty liver disease, and obesity.
- Musculoskeletal effects including osteoporosis, muscle weakness, and possibly further cartilage destruction.
- Nervous system issues of hyperactivity and lethargy.
- Vision problems including glaucoma and cataracts.
- Respiratory failures such as blood clots in the lungs.

can show these side effects. The higher the dose and the longer the therapy, the worse the problem. While these side effects are not harmful, they are upsetting to many owners. Therefore, when corticosteroids are used as part of the treatment of the arthritic dog, try to use the lowest doses possible for the shortest amount of time.

While the short-time side effects of corticosteroid therapy are not harmful per se, the long-term side effects are a totally different story. Because long-term side effects from corticosteroid therapy are numerous, I use them only when absolutely necessary.

To be fair, reports about whether corticosteroids actually destroy cartilage, thus worsening osteoarthritis, are conflicting. Since corticosteroids do decrease the abnormal formation of new bone and also decrease the destructive enzymes that occur with arthritis, some studies mention a positive benefit for their use. Other studies, especially where the corticosteroid was administered directly into the joint (called an intra-articular injection, which is commonly used in people with osteoarthritis), showed microscopic evidence of cartilage damage, even after a single intra-articular injection. Regardless of the potential damage to the joint, the number of other potential side effects suggests that more natural therapies should be used for the long-term treatment of arthritis in most pets.

Keep in mind that because the corticosteroids are potent anti-inflammatory and anti-pain medications, the decreased pain from the arthritis may encourage your dog to be more active. While increased activity is not in itself bad, activity should be restricted and monitored in the case of arthritis. Additionally, the increased activity coupled with the cartilage destruction, which may occur with corticosteroids, adds to the joint damage.

Safe Use of Steroid Therapy

Pets on long-term corticosteroid therapy must be monitored for side effects closely and frequently, usually every 2 to 3 months, by physical examination and blood and urine tests. As a rule, due to the side effects of corticosteroids, pets on long-term therapy are not expected to live as long as if they were not on these medications. It is distressing to see pets with osteoarthritis sentenced to a shortened life of corticosteroid therapy when no other therapies have been tried. Sure, there are very rare pets that do not respond to any conventional or complementary therapy that must take corticosteroids for life. And with appropriate dosing and monitoring, even these pets can live a decent quality of life when doctors are careful in handling these cases. Sadly, it's too easy for doctors and owners to give up and reach for the steroids any time a pet shows lameness. I would choose chronic therapy with corticosteroids for the arthritic pet only if all other treatments had failed after over a year of trying various safer therapies, and only if my other choice were euthanasia.

For pets that require corticosteroids or for owners who want to use them on a short-term basis, I usually can lower the dosage of corticosteroids when owners agree to try nutritional supplements and other complementary therapies for pets with arthritis. Complementary therapies, discussed in the next chapter, often allow us to use lower doses of the more potent corticosteroids.

NON-STEROIDAL ANTI-INFLAMMATORY MEDICATIONS

NON-STEROIDAL MEDICATIONS (NSAIDs) are the second group of medications commonly prescribed for people and dogs with various painful and inflammatory conditions,

COMMONLY USED CORTICOSTEROIDS

- Hydrocortisone
- Dexamethasone (AziumR)
- Prednisone
- Prednisolone

- Methylprednisolone (Solu-DeltaR)
- Betamethasone
- Triamcinolone

DURATION OF COMMONLY USED CORTICOSTEROIDS

Short Acting
Duration: Lasts 8 to 12 hours
- Hydrocortisone

Intermediate Acting
Duration: Lasts 12 to 36 hours*
- Prednisone
- Prednisolone
- Methylprednisolone
- Triamcinolone

Long Acting
Duration: Lasts longer than 36 hours
- Betamethasone
- Dexamethasone

*The actual duration depends upon a number of factors, including the specific formula. For example, the acetate and acetonid formulas are repositol, meaning they can act for weeks and last in the body for several months (very long acting). These preparations are overused in veterinary medicine and are the most harmful if used repeatedly.

including osteoarthritis. A number of these products are available, including aspirin, ibuprofen, naproxen, phenylbutazone, piroxicam, carprofen (Rimadyl), and etodolac (Ecto-Gesic). Even though it is often and incorrectly prescribed for this purpose, acetaminophen (Tylenol) is often prescribed for arthritis. However, it is not technically a non-steroidal medication as it has no anti-inflammatory properties.

Since dogs have shown greater toxicity (especially increased gastrointestinal side effects) with most of the human NSAID medications, whether they should be used in dogs for any reason is questionable. As a result of this increased sensitivity towards NSAID side effects, the pharmaceutical companies are developing products that are safer for our canine patients.

Side Effects of NSAIDs

Like corticosteroids, NSAIDs work by inhibiting the chemicals (prostaglandins) that cause pain and inflammation. They have the potential to produce a number of undesirable and potentially fatal side effects such as gastrointestinal bleeding, ulcers, kidney disease, liver disease, immune disease, destruction of articular cartilage, neurologic signs, behavior problems, and even death. We don't actually know the incidence of side effects in arthritic pets treated chronically (longer than one year) with non-steroidal medications. Because many of these medications are new, notably Rimadyl and EctoGesic, more studies are needed. However, here is an interesting statistic: In one study, four out of six dogs developed stomach ulcers after taking double the recommended dose of aspirin for 30 days. Unfortunately, little information is available on long-term side effects when dogs are given the recommended dose of aspirin.

COMMON NON-STEROIDAL MEDICATIONS

Only carprofen and etodolac have been approved for use in dogs. Although most of the other non-steroidal medications listed in this table are unsafe to use in dogs at any dosages, they are occasionally prescribed. Piroxicam is often prescribed for dogs with cancer to control pain. The use of piroxicam has rarely been associated with resolution of cancerous tumors. This list has been adapted from *The Natural Pharmacist: Everything You Need to Know about Arthritis,* by R. Hobbs and G. Bucco, 1999.

Medication	Brands
Aspirin	Ascriptin, Bayer
Carprofen	Rimadyl*
Celecoxib	Celebrex
Diclofenac Sodium	Arthrotec, Cataflam, Voltaren
Diflunisal	Dolobid
Etodolac	EctoGesic*
Fenoprofen	Nalfon
Flunixin Meglumine	Banamine
Flurbiprofen	Ansaid
Ibuprofen	Advil, Motrin, Nuprin
Indomethacin	Indocin
Ketoprofen	
Naproxen	Aleve, Anaprox, Naprosyn, Naprelan
Piroxicam	Feldene**
Phenylbutazone	Butazolidin
Salsalate	Salflex
Sulindac	Clinoril
Tolmetin sodium	Tolectin

*Approved for use in dogs
**Often prescribed for use in dogs with cancer for pain control. The use of piroxicam has rarely been associated with resolution of cancerous tumors.
Note: Most of these medications are unsafe to use in dogs at any dosages.

A CLOSER LOOK

While NSAIDs can be very useful in controlling pain and inflammation, like corticosteroids they have side effects, some more serious and dangerous than others, and these are discussed in the text. Here, I want to give you a short biochemistry lesson to help you understand how these side effects can occur.

COX stands for cyclooxygenase, which is another enzyme in the pathway that breaks down the arachidonic acid in the cell membranes of the joint into chemicals such as free radicals and various prostaglandins that damage the articular cartilage.

Two COX enzymes have been discovered to date: COX-1 and COX-2. COX-1, found in various tissues such as the stomach, intestines, and kidneys, serves an important role in maintaining health. When arachidonic acid is broken down by COX-1, good, anti-inflammatory prostaglandins are produced. These prostaglandins keep the kidneys functioning normally and help protect the stomach and intestinal tract against ulcers.

When arachidonic acid is broken down by COX-2, bad, pro-inflammatory prostaglandins are produced. These prostaglandins and other chemicals are harmful and contribute to

Gastrointestinal bleeding can lead to ulcers of the stomach and intestine and possibly to perforation of the stomach or intestines. This occurs because of prostaglandin inhibition. While a good effect of non-steroidal medications is inhibition of the prostaglandins that cause joint inflammation and pain side effects such as gastrointestinal ulcers and kidney disease that are seen in some patients taking NSAID medications. Drugs that selectively inhibit COX-2 but not COX-1 are most likely to result in fewer side effects and be safer for your dog. Right now the search is on in human medicine to find NSAIDs that inhibit COX-2 but not COX-1 and, soon, hopefully our veterinary patients will benefit from this research as well.

Non-steroidal medications that are selective for COX-2 may be safer than other non-steroidal medications.

Current NSAID medications available for veterinary patients inhibit both COX-1 and COX-2 to various degrees. Indomethacin and piroxicam have high COX-2-to-COX-1 ratios, and result in high incidences of gastrointestinal problems like bleeding and ulcers. Naproxen, ibuprofen, carprofen (Rimadyl) and etodolac (EctoGesic) have lower COX-2-to-COX-1 ratios and, as a result, have fewer gastrointestinal (GI) problems. Aspirin has a higher ratio but an intermediate incidence of GI problems, indicating that something else may be causing some of the side effects seen in dogs taking NSAIDs.

via COX-2 inhibition (see sidebar), the protective prostaglandins that are necessary to help prevent ulcers of the gastrointestinal tract are also inhibited via COX-1 inhibition.

These protective prostaglandins are needed to maintain the alkaline mucus barrier of the stomach, which prevents stomach acids from destroying the stomach lining. Inhibition of these protective prostaglandins decreases the protective mucus layer, making bleeding and ulceration more likely to occur.

Looking to human medicine for clues, here is some information from the package insert for Celebrex, a new nonsteroidal medication for people made by Pfizer and Searle. Keeping in mind that Celebrex is supposed to be a safer NSAID, targeting mainly the COX-2 enzyme, read this statement from the package insert:

> *Serious GI toxicity such as bleeding, ulceration, and perforation of the stomach, small intestine or large intestine, can occur at any time, with or without warning symptoms, in patients treated with NSAIDs. Only ⅕ (20 percent) of patients who develop serious upper GI adverse events on NSAID therapy are symptomatic. Upper GI ulcers … appear to occur in approximately 1 percent of patients treated for 3–6 months, and in about 2–4 of patients treated for one year.*

The insert did go on to state that in short-term studies on patients taking Celebrex for 3 to 6 months, only 0.04 percent experienced significant upper GI bleeding, although the significance of this finding is unknown. While it appears that this product (only used in humans for now) is possibly safer that other NSAIDs (which inhibit both COX-1 and COX-2), pay attention to the general warning signs listed in the insert regarding NSAID administration in general.

Only 20 percent of people *showed signs* of a serious GI side effect; the other 80 percent had serious side effects but *did not show signs!* Unfortunately, we don't have good studies in our pets to compare to this study, but I would assume the incidence of asymptomatic pet patients is similar to that of human patients.

Let's look at some of the information put out by Pfizer, manufacturer of not only Celebrex but the popular NSAID drug Rimadyl, commonly prescribed for dogs. This information is excerpted from the *Pfizer Animal Health Technical Bulletin,* "First-Year Clinical Experience with Rimadyl (carprofen): Assessment of Product Safety, May 1998" and "Update: Two Years (1997–1998) Clinical Experience with Rimadyl (carprofen) August, 1999."

Key Points
1. *More than 2.5 million dogs were treated with Rimadyl.*
2. *The reported rate of adverse reactions is low, approximately 0.2 percent, in 1997, and 0.18 percent in the 2-year study.*
3. *Approximately 70 percent of possible adverse drug events have been in older dogs.*
4. *Patient evaluation including physical examination and appropriate diagnostics is prudent before prescribing any medications.*
5. *When any medication is prescribed, owners should be informed of potential drug-related side effects and signs of drug tolerance.*

Let's look at the last three key points, which I believe are the most important.

Key point #3 deals with the fact that most reactions to Rimadyl occur in older dogs. This is not surprising for several reasons (some of which I'll discuss with the possible side effects of Rimadyl). First, most dogs with osteoarthritis are older dogs. Second, older pets are more likely to have drug reactions for two reasons: they have decreased ability to metabolize and excrete drugs from their bodies, and many older patients are taking multiple medications, which can interact with each other thus increasing the chances of a drug reaction. Third, many older pets have additional medical problems (such as kidney or liver disease), which may be undiagnosed at the time a medicine is prescribed. These added problems increase the chance of a drug reaction.

> Older pets are more likely to have drug reactions for two reasons: they have decreased ability to metabolize and excrete drugs from their bodies, and many older patients are taking multiple medications, which can interact with each other thus increasing the chances of a drug reaction

Key point #4 makes sense. Every patient receiving any medication should have a proper physical examination and diagnostic testing (blood and urine test for nonsteroidal medications such as Rimadyl will usually suffice). Unfortunately, the pet that receives the necessary diagnostics before chronic administration of Rimadyl is prescribed is rare. If Rimadyl is going to be administered for more than a short-term treatment (3- to 7-day maximum), it is imperative that your pet receive diagnostic testing to uncover anything wrong that may increase his risk of adverse drug reactions.

Key point #5 also makes sense. Owners must know about possible side effects so they can recognize the earliest signs of any side effects, stop the medication, and notify the doctor. Yet when it comes to Rimadyl, no owner has yet told me that her previous doctor discussed testing or side effects with her. Most owners are astonished to hear there are any side effects at all! This is no doubt due to the multi-million dollar advertising campaign put on by Pfizer to promote Rimadyl, suggesting that long-term treatment is now available to help restore your old pet back to his younger, more mobile self. In fairness to Pfizer, the ad briefly mentions that side effects can occur in pets taking NSAID medications. Yet based on my experience, obviously owners overlook this caution and their doctors neglect to point this out as well.

I would add a key point #6 to this list, which would state that any pet that must receive Rimadyl for long-term therapy should have ongoing examinations and diagnostics to allow early detection of any possible side effects. I require regular testing of pets that are receiving any medication on a long-term basis before the owner can refill the prescription! To do anything else is bad medicine and potential malpractice.

Here is Pfizer's recommendation for the use of Rimadyl in geriatric (6 years of age and older) dogs. Again, this is excerpted from the *Pfizer Animal Health Technical Bulletin*, "First-Year Clinical Experience with Rimadyl (carprofen): Assessment of Product Safety, May 1998."

- *Complete history and physical examination are necessary before prescribing Rimadyl.*
- *Definitive diagnosis should be determined so therapeutic response can be monitored.*
- *Baseline and repeat laboratory testing should be considered and are valuable in the geriatric dog.*

- *Follow-up communication between doctor and pet owner is important.*

- *Owners should be informed of clinical signs of drug intolerance (lack of appetite, vomiting, jaundice, and behavioral changes).*

- *Repeat laboratory values should be considered before refilling prescriptions.*

- *Recheck evaluations should be done after 2–4 weeks of treatment and then 3–6 months later if chronic treatment is needed.*

Kidney Disease   Kidney dysfunction may also occur due to prostaglandin inhibition as a result of NSAID administration. Dogs with underlying kidney disease, usually older pets, are at greater risk. Any time dehydration is present, the risk of kidney disease increases. Pre-treatment blood and urine testing can detect some but not all kidney problems.

Liver Disease   The most serious side effect seen in dogs taking Rimadyl is liver disease. Two subsets of "liver disease" were seen. In the first subset are dogs with elevated liver enzymes detected on a blood test. Most of these dogs are normal and elevated enzymes were only detected during routine monitoring. The second and more serious subset were dogs with signs of liver disease or liver failure; these dogs require intensive hospitalization, and death may result. One-third of all dogs in this class are Labrador Retrievers. This may represent a true breed predisposition or may simply reflect the fact that Labrador Retrievers are popular dogs and many of them have arthritis.

Immune diseases such as anemia, low platelet counts, and skin reactions have been seen in dogs undergoing NSAID treatment. Neurologic disease showing seizures, paralysis, and unsteadiness have been seen in a small number of dogs that take NSAIDs.

Behavioral Problems Aggression, depression, hyperactivity, and other behavioral problems can occur in pets taking Rimadyl or some other NSAIDs as well.

Drug Interaction NSAIDs can have dangerous interactions with other medications that can result in increased or decreased concentrations of the medications in the pet's blood, which may result in clinical disease. Drug interaction most likely occurs in pets taking medication for epilepsy such as phenobarbital or heart failure such as Lasix (furosemide), digoxin, and Enacard (enalapril and other ACE inhibitors).

Cartilage Damage Finally (and perhaps most importantly), as with steroids, many of the NSAIDs destroy cartilage. They do this by inhibiting the enzymes necessary for the multiplication of the chondrocytes and the synthesis of proteoglycans. Both Rimadyl and EctoGesic appear to cause less cartilage destruction than other NSAIDs. Some studies reveal no cartilage damage in the test tube, depending upon the dose administered. Some studies even suggest that a low dosage actually increased the glycosaminoglycans, indicating cartilage healing. What significance the test-tube tests have to your dog has yet to be determined.

I've used Rimadyl as the NSAID example since it was the first one and remains the one most commonly prescribed for dogs. Even though EctoGesic favors inhibition of the COX-2 enzyme, it can also cause any of these same side effects. So far, the good news about EctoGesic is that it is prescribed for once-a-day use—unlike Rimadyl, which is used twice daily.

I've talked with some doctors who have seen more GI side effects such as rectal bleeding in pets taking EctoGesic than in Rimadyl, although diarrhea and bleeding has also been reported to me by doctors prescribing Rimadyl. These doctors surmised that the increase in side effects may be due to the higher blood levels of EctoGesic that allow it to be given only once daily. At this point probably either medication can be used safely on a short-term basis as long as the pet is monitored for diarrhea, blood in the feces, and any other side effects.

To date I have not seen or heard of any specific liver problems in pets taking EctoGesic. Liver problem side effects are most common in Labrador Retrievers taking Rimadyl, which may indicate that EctoGesic is a better choice for Labs with arthritis.

Even these two medications that are considered safe have only been tested up to 12 months of continuous use, yet a number of dogs are taking these medications for many years. Time will tell whether more side effects appear in pets taking these NSAIDs for longer than the year tested. Also consider that the safety margin in these products is narrow. For example, quoting from the EctoGesic package insert:

Elevated dose levels of EctoGesic at 2.7 times the maximum daily dose causes gastrointestinal ulceration, vomiting, and fecal blood and weight loss.

Yet, EctoGesic is supposed to be a "safe" NSAID. Ideally the first prescribed dose should start at the low end of the dosage range to minimize side effects. It is important to care-

POSSIBLE SIDE EFFECTS IN DOGS TREATED WITH CORTICOSTEROIDS OR NON-STEROIDAL MEDICATIONS

- Gastrointestinal Problems: GI bleeding, ulceration, perforation, pancreatitis
- Kidney Disease
- Liver Disease: Elevated liver enzymes, liver failure
- Immune Diseases: Anemia, low platelet counts, and skin reactions
- Neurologic Disease: Seizures, paralysis, unsteadiness
- Behavioral Problems: Aggression, depression, hyperactivity
- Drug Interactions: Phenobarbital, Lasix (furosemide), digoxin, and Enacard (enalapril and other ACE inhibitors).
- Cartilage Damage

fully follow the prescribed dosages if your pet must take these NSAIDs for even short-term use.

There Is Good News, Too!

While it is tempting to swear off using NSAID medication, that is not my goal in presenting this information to you.

Here is some of the good news about NSAID therapy:

First, the incidence of side effects is extremely low for pets taking Rimadyl or EctoGesic, approximately 0.18 percent. I have not seen any side effects at all when using these products in my practice. However, I carefully screen my patients and only use the medications on a short-term, as-needed basis. Time will tell just how safe these medications are for long-term usage.

NSAID medications are best used at the lowest dose needed to maintain patient comfort, and only on an "as-needed" basis.

Second, compared to aspirin and other NSAIDs, both Rimadyl and EctoGesic have fewer side effects. For example, only minor GI erosions were seen in dogs taking Rimadyl or EctoGesic, whereas all dogs receiving aspirin had GI hemorrhages. Therefore, when NSAID therapy is needed for short-term pain relief, either Rimadyl or EctoGesic would be preferred over aspirin therapy in the arthritic dog. NSAID medications are best used at the lowest dose needed to maintain patient comfort, and only on an "as-needed" basis.

Safe Use of NSAIDs

Despite the potential side effects, non-steroidal medications can be used safely and effectively under a doctor's supervision, most often for short-term pain management. I often use them for temporary relief while waiting to see results from our complementary therapies. This holistic approach allows me to combine the use of both conventional and comple-

mentary therapies safely to the benefit of the pet while minimizing side effects.

I believe NSAIDs can be safely and effectively used for 5
to 7 days in pets not taking any other medications and in
pets without other diseases after a careful history, examination, and laboratory testing have been done.

For the long term, use NSAIDs on your dog only if all
other treatments have failed and when you are aware of the
potential side effects. You must agree to have your dog monitored every 2 to 3 months for side effects. Also ask about
GI-protective medications (see below) that may be used to
decrease GI side effects. In effect, we try to make the patient
comfortable and have a good quality of life at the risk of
causing side effects and even death in that pet.

The best advice I can offer about using non-steroidal
medications in pets comes in the form of a quote from
David Bennett and Christopher May in *Textbook of Veterinary Internal Medicine,* 4th ed.:

> *Blanket therapy with anti-inflammatory drugs is
> a poor substitute for a well-designed program of
> management.*

You should never use any drug without a doctor's approval. Over-the-counter human anti-arthritis medications
and analgesics should never be used without doctor supervision as many of these products can be fatal in pets.

For example, in dogs, acetaminophen can be extremely
toxic and even fatal. Toxicity of the drug can cause liver and
kidney failure. Additionally, while acetaminophen is a good
pain killer and helps control fever, it is not a true anti-inflammatory drug. Therefore, while some dogs may receive a bit

of pain relief with this drug, it is not the best choice for the treatment of osteoarthritis.

Other NSAIDs such as Naprosyn are extremely toxic and can cause severe clinical signs including death. While I will often use an NSAID such as piroxicam in pets with severe pain or cancer, I am careful to monitor these pets and choose other therapies when appropriate. Since Rimadyl and EctoGesic are manufactured specifically for dogs and are safer than most of the NSAIDs made for people, use these first when they are indicated and follow the guidelines outlined in this chapter. If your pet acts sick while taking any NSAIDs, stop the medication and contact your veterinarian at once.

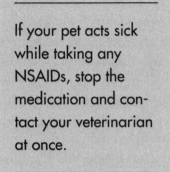

If your pet acts sick while taking any NSAIDs, stop the medication and contact your veterinarian at once.

Doctors who prescribe potent non-steroidal therapy may also prescribe other drugs in an attempt to decrease the possibility of gastrointestinal ulceration and perforation. The one drug shown to be effective in reducing the incidence of GI bleeding and ulcers is misoprostol (Cytotec). Despite the fact that many doctors prescribe cimetidine (Tagamet), this medication has not been shown to effectively reduce GI side effects in pets or people taking NSAID medications.

While the use of Cytotec may be necessary for some pets, those who prefer holistic therapy do not find the use of multiple drugs to help control the pain and inflammation of arthritis particularly appealing. Aversion to using multiple drugs makes complementary therapies (the subject of the next chapter) particularly attractive to pet owners.

SAFE USE OF NSAIDS IN ARTHRITIC PETS

- A proper diagnosis is essential before considering chronic therapy with NSAIDs.
- NSAIDs are most safely used on as "as-needed" basis.
- The lowest effective dose should be given.
- Other safer complementary therapies should serve as the basis for long-term pain relief and cartilage healing for most pets.
- NSAIDs should only be considered for chronic therapy after all other treatments have failed.
- Pets taking NSAID therapy for chronic arthritis relief must have a physical examination, and blood and urine testing done every 2 to 3 months to monitor for side effects. This is especially true in geriatric patients (dogs over 6 years old) and all Labrador Retrievers.
- If your pet acts sick while taking Rimadyl or EctoGesic, stop the medication and contact your veterinarian at once.

SURGERY

MOST PEOPLE DON'T think of surgery as a potential cure for osteoarthritis as surgery can't really cure osteoarthritis. However, in some conditions, surgery can prevent osteoarthritis. Surgery can fix unstable joints before the joint even becomes arthritic.

Fritz is a very energetic 6-month-old male Golden Retriever puppy. Under anesthesia during surgery to neuter him, I evaluated his hip joints in two ways. First, I physically attempted to pop his hips out of joint. In dogs with normal hips, this is impossible to do. In Fritz, however, the hips readily popped out of joint. (Don't worry: the procedure is not painful and the hips readily pop back into their sockets at the completion of the evaluation!) While Fritz was still under anesthesia, we shot a radiograph of the hips. This must also be done under sedation to allow full extension of the legs, otherwise the test is not truly valid. Unfortunately, Fritz had hip dysplasia. Due to his young age and severe signs, he was a perfect candidate for corrective surgery to replace his hips. After surgery he took short-term non-steroidal medications to relieve post-operative pain and nutritional supplements to help his hips heal with minimal pain and inflammation, and to allow the cartilage to heal as well. After surgery to replace his hips, he recovered quickly and should lead a full life with new hips and never develop arthritis of the hips as he gets older.

In dogs like Fritz, with early diagnosis and intervention, surgery can resolve the problem long before the joint even becomes arthritic. In the older pet recently diagnosed with hip dysplasia as a cause of lameness, total hip replacement surgery will often cure the problem.

Another example of surgery preventing osteoarthritis occurs in the dog with a damaged cruciate ligament of the knee. This criss-crossed ligament is easily torn in active dogs and people. And for pets and people, corrective surgery can often prevent arthritis that would inevitably occur.

For those pets with problems that can be corrected or prevented by surgery, owners should strongly consider this alternative. Supplements can be used to aid healing without side effects.

I often see pets with severe osteoarthritis secondary to hip dysplasia. In some of these cases, surgery is desirable, but for some reason immediate surgery is not an option. Some of these pets might be too small for a total hip replacement. In other situations, owners must delay the surgery until it becomes affordable. For these pets, holistic care, including nutritional, acupuncture, or homeopathy, is beneficial while awaiting a surgical cure.

YOUR HEALING GOALS

THE BEST THERAPY for dogs with osteoarthritis has these goals: to relieve pain and inflammation, heal the destroyed cartilage by supplying it with glycosaminoglycans, and produce minimal or no side effects. Your goals in helping your pet are to relieve its pain, slow down the progression of the arthritis, and, if possible, actually help the joint to heal. Most conventional therapies do a great job of treating inflammation and pain but rarely help the joint to heal. In many cases, these anti-inflammatory therapies actually cause more cartilage damage as time progresses. Wouldn't it be great if therapies could relieve the pain and inflammation associated with osteoarthritis without causing the side effects seen with conventional medications? Many complementary therapies relieve pain and inflammation plus actually supply nutrients to help the cartilage heal and slow down the destructive forces of nature that act to destroy the injured joint. These ancient and innovative methods are presented in the next chapter.

CHAPTER SUMMARY

• The goal of therapy must be to relieve the pain and help solve the problem with minimal side effects.

• The two most common classes of conventional medications for osteoarthritis are corticosteroids and NSAIDs.

• Corticosteroids and NSAIDs help relieve pain and fight inflammation.

• The side effects of steroids and NSAIDs include gastrointestinal, kidney, liver, neurological, and behavior problems plus additional cartilage damage.

• Surgery is an option for preventing osteoarthritis caused by hip dysplasia and cruciate injuries and to "cure" it through total hip replacement.

· 5 ·

Complementary Therapies for Arthritis

Nutritional and Chondroprotective Supplements

A S PEOPLE TURN to more natural, holistic care for their own bodies, many are choosing the same approach for their pets. The most familiar complementary treatments for pets with arthritis are nutritional supplements, chondroprotective supplements that help heal the damaged cartilage, herbal treatments, acupuncture, magnetic therapy, and homeopathy.

A number of other complementary therapies are available, but examining in detail all purported approaches is beyond the scope of this book. Therefore, I will concentrate on the most popular complementary treatments for the pet with arthritis.

Keep in mind that, often, several different types of complementary therapies can be used simultaneously in an effort to maximize the chance of a successful outcome. Using multiple products may also decrease the need for conventional treatments. There's no way I can say what you should use for your pet, since each pet has individual needs. Emphasizing the holistic approach, work with your own veterinarian to determine which course of therapy is best for your pet.

NUTRITIONAL SUPPLEMENTS

A NUMBER OF nutritional supplements are available that may benefit the pet with arthritis. These include enzymes, green foods, fatty acids, and health formulas that contain antioxidants. Other supplements are cartilage protective; these include shark cartilage and products containing glucosamine and chondroitin, the building blocks of cartilage. Either type of supplement can be useful by itself or in conjunction with conventional therapies, depending upon each pet's individual needs. The dosage of conventional medications can be reduced for many pets that are taking supplements, with the ultimate goal being to wean them off all medications.

> While you can use many great supplements for treating arthritis in pets, there is no "ideal" supplement and supplements are not cure-alls.

While you can use many great supplements for treating arthritis in pets, there is no "ideal" supplement and supplements are not cure-alls. No one supplement is perfect for every pet in every situation, and deciding which to use is not easy. As a veterinarian, I certainly have favorite products that I have used with success in a variety of medical conditions. If one product doesn't produce the desired effect, your doctor has a choice of other products he can try. Unless the product contains drugs or chemical fillers, there are usually no side effects when these products are used as directed. Because the supplement industry is young and not stringently regulated, you should only use nutritional supplements under veterinary supervision.

Often, veterinarians must try several products before they obtain a positive response. Commonly, I will use several supplements to get an additive effect and see results. It may take 2 to 3 months before positive effects are seen from supplements as your dog's body "detoxifies" and begins assimilating more nutrients.

In choosing a supplement, I believe a good supplement should meet the following criteria:

- The supplement should be safe and not harm your pet.

- The supplement should be palatable so that your pet will ingest it.

- The supplement must be cost effective. Of course, if the supplement can prevent or cure disease you will save money in veterinary expenses over the life of your pet.

- The supplement should be easy for you to administer. Many medications prescribed by doctors are never given to the pet since owners experience difficulty giving the dog or cat a pill or liquid. Supplements come in a pill, liquid, or chewable tablet form, or as a powder to be sprinkled on the pet's food. The powdered form may be the easiest to give pets.

- The supplement should not interfere with other therapies that may be necessary for the pet.

- The correct dosage of the supplement should be known. This requirement of the ideal nutritional supplement is the hardest to meet. Many supplements are recommended based upon anecdotal evidence and clinical experience but lack any hard scientific studies to establish ideal dosages. This doesn't mean the supplements can't be used effectively. Many supplements for which the "best" dosage is not known are often used safely and effectively to treat arthritic dogs. Because studies that establish proper use of many supplements are lacking, you must work closely with your doctor to review the information on available supplements to find the most appropriate dosage possible. When supplements fail to work, the simple reason may be that the dosage was incorrect.

When supplements work, they allow you to reduce the dosage of medications that have the potential to cause serious side effects. Holistic doctors (myself included) have no problem trying products based on anecdotal information, but we encourage additional scientific studies to determine the true effectiveness of any complementary therapy. More research is needed to determine the true effectiveness of enzymes, green foods, fatty acids, and health-blend formulas in the treatment of osteoarthritis. I encourage you to talk with your pet's doctor about trying any supplement. While such supplements are safe and cause no side effects, you want to be sure that the doctor is aware of every aspect of your dog's treatment.

Keep the above ideas in mind as you consider the more commonly used nutritional supplements that might help your pet with osteoarthritis.

Enzymes

Cellular processes, digestion, and absorption of dietary nutrients are dependent upon the proper enzymes. The pancreas produces the enzymes amylase, lipase, and various proteases. Amylase is used for digesting carbohydrates, lipase is used for digesting fats, and proteases are used by the body to digest proteins.

Once properly digested by pancreatic enzymes, dietary nutrients can be absorbed.

Enzymes found in food contribute to digestion and nutrient absorption as well. Natural, raw diets contain a number of chemicals, including enzymes not found in processed diets. Food enzymes are broken down in the presence of temperatures in the range of 120 to 160 degrees Fahrenheit and in the presence of freezing temperatures, which means that processing often alters the nutrients found in a pet's food, depleting it of important nutrients and enzymes. Supplying additional enzymes through the use of supplements can replenish enzymes absent in processed foods. Even pets on natural raw diets can often benefit from additional enzymes, which is why such diets are often recommended as a supplement.

> Nothing is magical about enzymes themselves. They work by liberating essential nutrients from the pet's diet.

Nothing is magical about enzymes themselves. They work by liberating essential nutrients from the pet's diet. While we do not know all the wonderful things enzymes do, we do know that certain enzyme supplements can increase the absorption of essential vitamins, minerals, and certain fatty acids from the diet. Increased absorption of zinc, selenium, vitamin B6, and linoleic acid have been detected after taking plant enzyme supplements. In some pets with osteoarthritis, the increased absorption of these various nutrients helps to relieve the pain and inflammation that occur. Unfortunately, while enzyme supplements do make the pet more comfortable, they do not actually heal the cartilage. To do that, we must use supplements containing glucosamine and chondroitin, as you will read below.

Doctors can prescribe pancreatic enzymes, microbial enzymes, or plant enzymes. Plant enzymes are the preferred enzymes to use as supplements for the arthritic pet because they are active over a much wider pH range than pancreatic enzymes. Plants contain the enzyme cellulase. Dogs and cats do not normally have cellulase in their bodies, which is why they can only digest some of the plant material in their diets. Enzyme supplements that contains cellulase in addition to the normal lipase, amylase, and proteases found in many supplements seem to be advantageous to pets with medical problems such as arthritis because they liberate zinc and other chemicals that might be bound by fiber.

Enzyme supplements are inexpensive, safe, and easy to administer in pill or powder form. Your doctor can help you decide which product is best for your pet's condition.

Green Foods

Green foods most commonly include barley grass, spirulina, alfalfa, and algae. The intent of using these products is to duplicate the grass that wild dogs ingest when they kill herbivorous prey animals and eat their intestinal contents. Green foods contain a variety of healthy nutrients.

These nutrients help prevent and treat illnesses caused by an imbalance of minerals, enzymes, and vitamins in processed-food diets.

The enzymes contained in green foods are not just those that can aid in digestion and absorption of nutrients from the diet but may also assist in reducing oxidative injury to the damaged cartilage. For example, barley grass contains large amounts of vitamins C, A, B1, B2, B6, and E; biotin; folic acid; choline; pantothenic acid; nicotinic acid; iron; chlorophyll; potassium; calcium; magnesium; manganese; zinc; proteins; and enzymes. Chlorophyll may assist the body in healing due to an anti-inflammatory effect. Because green foods act as anti-inflammatory supplements, they can be useful in combination with other supplements for dogs with arthritis.

Oral Fatty Acids

Fats in the form of fatty acids have recently become a popular supplement among most veterinarians, not just those interested in holistic care. We are, in fact, just beginning to see that fatty acids may be valuable in a variety of conditions. Fatty acids were first purported to work in some pets with allergic dermatitis, and are in fact an essential part of the pet's diet. They are also prescribed for pets with dry, flaky skin and dull coats. Recently, they have been advocated in pets with kidney disease, elevated cholesterol, and arthritis.

When discussing fatty acids, we're not just talking about adding some vegetable oil to the pet's diet to get a nice, shiny coat. The fatty acids of most concern are the omega-3 and omega-6 fatty acids. Omega-9 fatty acids have no known use in treating pets. Omega-3 fatty acids—eicosapentaenoic acid (EPA) and docosahexaenoic acid (DHA)—are derived from fish oils of coldwater fish such as salmon and trout, and flax seed. Omega-6 fatty acids—linoleic acid (LA) and gamma-linolenic acid (GLA)—are derived from the oils of seeds such as evening primrose, black currant, and borage. Often fatty acids are added to the diet with other supplements to attain an additive effect. This is especially common in arthritic dogs, as fatty acid supplements by themselves usually fail to relieve pain and lameness.

Remember, arthritis is caused by an inflammation of the joint. Since the same enzymes metabolize both omega-3 and omega-6 fatty acids, and since metabolism of the omega-6 fatty acids tends to cause inflammation by supplying a large amount of omega-3 fatty acids, we favor the production of

A CLOSER LOOK

Cell membranes in the joint contain phospholipids. When the membrane is injured, an enzyme acts on the phospholipids in the cell membranes to produce fatty acids including arachidonic acid (an omega-6 fatty acid) and eicosapentaenoic acid (an omega-3 fatty acid). Further metabolism of the arachidonic acid and eicosapentaenoic acid by additional enzymes (the lipooxygenase and cyclooxygenase pathways) produce chemicals called eicosanoids. The eicosanoids produced by metabolism of arachidonic acid are pro-inflammatory and cause inflammation, suppress the immune system, and cause platelets to aggregate and clot. Many disorders are due to overproduction of the eicosanoids responsible for producing inflammation, including arthritis. The eicosanoids produced by metabolism of eicosapentaenoic acid are non-inflammatory, not immunosuppressive, and help inhibit platelets from clotting.

In general, the products of omega-3 (specifically EPA) and one omega-6 fatty acid (DGLA) are less inflammatory than the products of arachidonic acid (another omega-6 fatty acid). By changing dietary fatty acid consumption, the eicosanoid production changes right at the cellular level, decreasing inflammation within the body. By providing the proper anti-inflammatory fatty acids, we can use fatty acids as an anti-inflammatory substance. However, since the products of omega-6 fatty acid metabolism (specifically arachidonic acid) are not the sole cause of the inflammation in pets with arthritis, fatty acid therapy is rarely effective as the sole therapy but is used as an additional therapy to achieve an additive effect.

non-inflammatory chemicals. Therefore, supplementing the diet with omega-3 fatty acids may relieve inflammation in the arthritic joints.

Note: Flaxseed oil is a popular source of alpha-linoleic acid (ALA), an omega-3 fatty acid that is ultimately converted to EPA and DHA. However, many species of pets (probably including dogs) and some people cannot convert ALA to these other more active non-inflammatory omega-3 fatty acids. In one study of people (Hobbs and Bucco, 1999), flaxseed oil was ineffective in reducing symptoms or raising levels of EPA and DHA. Therefore, because supplementation with EPA and DHA is important, flaxseed oil is not recommended as a fatty acid supplement for pets.

> Supplementing the diet with omega-3 fatty acids may relieve inflammation in the arthritic joints.

Some evidence in people (which has been extrapolated to pets) shows that supplementing omega-3 fatty acids in the form of fish oil provided relief from pain associated with rheumatoid arthritis. Twelve double-blind placebo-controlled studies showed a significant reduction of symptoms with minimal side effects in people with rheumatoid arthritis (Hobbs and Bucco, 1999). In another study, reduction of symptoms correlated with doses of the fatty acid supplement. The group taking the higher dose of supplement had a greater decrease in signs than the group taking the lower dosage.

However, while osteoarthritis is common in pets, rheumatoid arthritis is very rare. Still there may be a synergistic effect between the fatty acids and other anti-arthritic supplements, and fatty acid supplementation is recommended for pets with osteoarthritis.

Because of their anti-inflammatory effects, I routinely add large doses of fatty acids to other supplements in treating arthritic dogs. (By "large doses," I mean two to four times the label dose, as the label dose on most products is suspected to be too low to provide anti-inflammatory effects.) As with the other supplements, using fatty acids will often allow doctors to lower the dosages of drugs such as corticosteroids or non-steroidal medications.

Since processed foods have increased omega-6 fatty acids and decreased omega-3 fatty acids, if your dog eats processed food, adding omega-3 fatty acid supplements is probably good idea.

However, while many doctors (including me) use fatty acids for a variety of medical problems, there is considerable debate about the use of fatty acids as a treatment for arthritis and other health problems (such as allergies, heart disease, and kidney disease) in pets. One part of the debate concerns what dosage to use for treating pets. As noted above most doctors, including myself, recommend using at least two to four times the label dose of fatty acid to maximize the anti-inflammatory action.

Research on using fatty acids for the treatment of allergies indicates that the label dose is ineffective. The same theory probably holds true for treating arthritis, but the research is lacking. The dosages used for people that showed effectiveness in the studies quoted were 1.4 to 2.8 grams of GLA per day, or 1.7 grams of EPA and 0.9 grams of DHA per day. This amount is difficult for people to obtain from the supplements currently available. If this were shown to be the correct dosage for pets, a 50-pound dog would require ten or more fatty acids capsules per day to obtain a similar dosage, depending upon which supplement (of the many choices on the market) is used.

Another concern is the correct fatty acid to use. Should we use just omega-3 (EPA and DHA) fatty acids, or combine them with omega-6 (GLA) fatty acids? Is there an ideal ratio of omega-6 to omega-3 fatty acids? The ideal dietary ratio seems to be 5:1 of omega-6:omega-3 fatty acids, although this is also debated. Whether or not this dietary ratio is "ideal" for the treatment of arthritis also lacks research.

Finally, the method of distributing the fatty acid is also in question. Fatty acids can be provided in capsules, liquids, or by adding the "ideal" ratio of omega-6 and omega-3 fatty acids to food. There are, in fact, diets constructed with this "ideal" ratio. If you do not like giving your pet medication, or if your pet won't take the fatty acid supplements easily, you might be wise to try some of the medically formulated diets available from your pet's doctor that contain the fatty acids. These diets, often prescribed as anti-inflammatory diets for pets with allergies, may be useful as a part of the therapy for arthritic pets.

The bottom line is that we still have many questions regarding the use of fatty acid therapy as part of the treatment for arthritic pets. We need more research to determine the effectiveness of the fatty acids in the treatment of arthritis. Until we obtain definitive answers, you will need to work with your doctors to determine the use of these supplements for your pet.

Health Formulas

A number of products that contain a variety of ingredients, including barley grass, wheat, rice, enzymes, fatty acids, vitamins, minerals, seaweed, and alfalfa, claim to be health formulas. We don't really know why these compounds often seem effective for treating pets with arthritis. Obviously, they supply some nutrient that is missing from the dog's diet, most likely antioxidants, vitamins, and minerals. Like fatty acid supplements, it may be that they interfere with the production of pro-inflammatory compounds. Possibly they also supply nutrients for the chondrocytes that produce substances to help heal and maintain a normal joint. Because so many different products are available, it would be wise to discuss whatever products you may discover with your pet's veterinarian.

Antioxidants

Certain vitamins and minerals function in the body to reduce oxidation. Oxidation is a chemical process that occurs within the body's cells. After oxidation occurs, certain by-products such as peroxides and "free radicals" accumulate. These cellular by-products are toxic to the cells and surrounding tissue. The body removes these by-products by producing additional chemicals called antioxidants that combat these oxidizing chemicals. Antioxidants neutralize the harmful by-products of cellular oxidation, including peroxides and free radicals.

In disease, excess oxidation can occur and the body's normal antioxidant abilities are overwhelmed. This is where supplying antioxidants can help. By giving your pet's body extra antioxidants, you can neutralize the harmful by-products of cellular oxidation.

You can use any of several antioxidants to supplement treatment of your arthritic pet. Most commonly, we prescribe the antioxidant vitamins A, C, and E, and the minerals selenium, manganese, and zinc. Other antioxidants include superoxide dismutase, glutathione, cysteine, coenzyme Q10, ginkgo biloba, bilberry, grape seed extract, and pycnogenol (an antioxidant that is promoted as an anti-arthritis agent in people, which may also be helpful for relieving pain and inflammation in arthritic pets).

Pycnogenol is a group of chemicals from the bark of pine trees native to southern France and is a mixture of bioflavonoids (also called proanthocyanidins, bioflavonoids are plant compounds that have multiple health benefits including antioxidation). These bioflavonoids inhibit the prostaglandins that cause inflammation and allergic responses. In addition to its use to help control arthritis in people, pycnogenol is also suggested for patients suffering from Adult Attention Deficit Disorder.

One source suggests that pycnogenol seems to work by enhancing the effects of another antioxidant, vitamin C. Other research suggests that the bioflavonoids can work independently of other antioxidants. As is the case with many supplements, there probably is an additive effective when multiple antioxidants are combined. People taking pycnogenol often report feeling better and having more energy, a positive side effect that may possibly occur in pets as well.

Bioflavanoids isolated from grape seed are also recommended for arthritic disorders for their anti-inflammatory effect.

Can antioxidants such as vitamin C actually prevent arthritis and skeletal problems in pets? Pet owners who want to prevent the common problem of hip dysplasia and secondary osteoarthritis in their puppies frequently ask this question. What does the research show?

Currently there are two conflicting sources of information dealing with this topic.

In the chapter "Developmental Orthopedics: Nutritional Influences in the Dog" *(Textbook of Veterinary Internal Medicine, 4th ed.,* W.B. Saunders, Co, 1999), Dr. Daniel Richardson cites one study that looks at this issue. Eight litters of German Shepherd puppies from known dysplastic parents or from dogs who had previously produced puppies with dysplasia were studied. The female dogs were given sodium ascorbate daily during pregnancy, and the puppies also received sodium ascorbate until they were 2 years of age. No dysplasia was seen in any of the puppies, although no radiographic studies or long-term follow-up was done. Dr. Richardson concluded that there is no evidence that vitamin C supplementation prevents hip dysplasia. To substantiate this claim, he argues that if vitamin C deficiency causes hip dysplasia, why are other joints spared? Finally, since dogs make their own vitamin C and do not have a dietary requirement for it, how can they develop a deficiency?

Dr. Wendell Belfield presents the other side of the argument in *Complementary and Alternative Veterinary Medicine: Principles and Practice* (Mosby Yearbook, 1997).

> Since vitamin C is a safe vitamin, incorporating it into a regimen to help patients with arthritis is not harmful and may offer help.

Dr. Belfield was the source of the study of the eight litters of German Shepherd puppies mentioned above. He believes that vitamin C can be used to prevent and treat pets with hip dysplasia and other joint conditions, including osteochondrosis and osteoarthritis.

What then is the truth? I believe that we need many controlled studies to determine the effectiveness, if any, of using only antioxidants to prevent and treat joint diseases. Since vitamin C is made by dogs yet not required in their diet, it is difficult to imagine a true deficiency occurring. Still, it is certainly possible that additional vitamin C may be helpful in healing or preventing joint problems. (Some of the common chondroprotective supplements include added vitamin C for this purpose.) While Dr. Belfield's

RAW FOODS AND
GLANDULAR SUPPLEMENTS

Raw food and glandular therapy involves giving the pet whole raw foods or glandular products to treat diseases. Glandular supplements are produced from cattle, swine, or sheep, and are concentrated by specific processes with high biochemical activity that can elicit specific nutritional or biochemical activity. Raw foods or natural vitamins are processed whole foods that supply all the biochemical components of the raw food, rather than just a single chemical fraction of a vitamin or mineral.

For example, instead of giving a pet chemically produced vitamin C, a raw food product would supply vitamin C in its natural state to the pet. Or instead of giving a pet chemically produced thyroid hormone, the doctor would prescribe a glandular product made from the thyroid gland of an animal.

research is impressive, further studies are indicated to document his findings, including radiographic studies of the pets and long-term follow-up to see whether problems develop over the life of the pets. Still, since vitamin C is a safe vitamin, incorporating it into a regimen to help patients with arthritis is not harmful and may offer help.

A number of studies show the benefit of providing vitamins, minerals, and hormones in their raw, natural state. For example, many studies indicate that when "synthetic vitamins are substituted for diets high in fresh fruits and vegetables, the protection against disease is lost and evidence shows reverses." (Frost, 1997) One older study from 1942 showed that people suffering from scurvy, a vitamin C deficiency, healed when given either fresh vitamin C (in the form of lemon juice) or synthetic ascorbic acid, but that those getting the natural vitamin C in the lemon juice healed more quickly than did those receiving synthetic ascorbic acid.

Another more recent study reported in the July 22, 1994 issue of *The New England Journal of Medicine* showed that synthetic antioxidants were not effective against recurrence of benign growths of the colon. Yet other studies have shown that diets high in natural antioxidants and other phytochemicals (vegetables and fruits) did have protection against colon cancer.

Proponents of natural raw foods suggest that these findings are due to the presence of phytochemicals, the numerous compounds present in the whole plant. Using this theory, it is not just synthetic vitamin C or ascorbic acid (a component of vitamin C) that is helpful, but rather the entire plant, which contains the entire complex molecule of vitamin C plus a number of other phytochemicals.

Studies have shown the following with regard to glandular products:

- There is an active accumulation of the injected cells or their constituents by the target tissues.

- There is a more rapid uptake of the corresponding injected cells in traumatized (diseased) organs than in normal organs, which may indicate an increased requirement by the diseased organs.

- There are tissue-specific effects of injected or implanted tissues on the corresponding tissues of the recipient (for example, thyroid cells given to animals with thyroid disease results in accelerated regeneration of the thyroid gland).

- The oral route of administration may be preferred due to a longer-lived effect.

- As in the case with raw foods (discussed below), glandular preparations contain not only the active substance (hormone) but a variety of substances with biologic activity, many of which have not been identified.

With raw foods, the concept is simple: don't provide simply a chemical vitamin or mineral but rather all the substances that may be included with the food. In conditions that may benefit from additional antioxidants, including arthritis, the sources of antioxidants in raw foods and glandular products may be preferred to chemically processed vitamins and minerals due to the number of phytochemicals. Synthetic vitamins and minerals may be of use in pets, but their use should not take priority over the natural vitamins and minerals in raw foods and glandular products.

One company has produced supplements for people that may also be prescribed for pets. Standard Process is a company founded on the belief of the superior value of vitamins and minerals in their whole raw food states when compared to synthetic products. For the treatment of osteoarthritis, the following supplements produced by Standard Process are recommended: Catalyn, Calcium Lactate, Calcifood, Cataplex B/C/G, Thymex, Ligaplex I, and Ligaplex II. A simplified protocol would use Catalyn and Ligaplex I and II.

While much research shows that these whole raw foods may be preferable to synthetic vitamins, many doctors who practice complementary therapies use synthetic vitamins with good success. The best conclusion I can reach is this:

- Feed your pets a good wholesome diet that is free of by-products and preservatives.

- Feed pets whole raw food supplements for maintenance and disease treatment.

- Use synthetic vitamins as directed by your doctor if needed for additional treatment.

CHONDROPROTECTIVE SUPPLEMENTS

WHEN WE TALK about chondroprotective agents, we're talking about "cartilage-protective" compounds. Unlike corticosteroids and other medications, these products actually help the cartilage rebuild and repair itself. In essence, they are "cartilage-friendly" products. These compounds also help relieve pain and inflammation. Chondroprotective agents can be given orally or by injection, often both forms in the severely arthritic and pain pet.

Optimum functioning of the joints is important for pain-free movements by the pet. While any pet can exhibit lameness or arthritis, the older pet is more commonly affected. Articular cartilage, cartilage that lines the joints, must remain healthy to allow the pet to function to its maximum capability. The articular cartilage acts as a shock absorber for the joint, providing a smooth surface between bones to eliminate bone-on-bone contact. As the cartilage is destroyed, bony surfaces contact and irritate each other, causing pain, inflammation, and reduced activity. While corticosteroids and certain non-steroidal medications certainly relieve the pain and inflammation, they further destroy the articular cartilage, making a bad situation even worse.

Cartilage is made of cells called chondrocytes, which make a matrix of molecules that add to the strength of the cartilage. This matrix consists of collagen, a protein that connects tissues, and substances called proteoglycans. These proteoglycans are made of glycosaminoglycans (GAGS) and hyaluronic acid. Surrounding the cartilage, and bathing the joint, is joint (synovial) fluid. Cartilage is a tough material that protects the underlying bones and acts as a shock absorber for the joints during movement. A certain amount of wear and tear on the joint cartilage is normal. The various cells and fluids are constantly being broken down and synthesized. It is important that the cartilage receive proper nutrition, especially when damaged and inflamed. Chondroprotective agents seek to replenish the raw materials that are essential for the healing and synthesis of cartilage, its matrix, and joint fluid.

Various products, each supplying different nutritional products, are available to assist in relieving inflammation and helping damaged cartilage to heal. The following ingredients may be included in the various nutritional chondroprotective products. Although each doctor has a "favorite" product, your doctor may suggest trying a different product if one doesn't help your pet. Keep in mind that these products have no harmful side effects such as those often encountered with long-term use of corticosteroids or non-steroidal medications.

You can choose from many chondroprotective supplements. If one doesn't help your pet, your doctor may suggest trying a different product.

Bovine Cartilage
Bovine cartilage has proven useful in relieving pain and inflammation in human patients with osteoarthritis and

rheumatoid arthritis; increased joint mobility was also noted. In dogs treated with bovine cartilage, good results were seen in the treatment of degenerative disk disease and some spinal disorders. Like shark cartilage, bovine cartilage is high in glycosaminoglycans that can help the body repair damaged joints. Since shark cartilage was found to be 1,000 times more times effective in preventing new blood vessel growth, it has replaced bovine cartilage as a supplement for many doctors. The recommended dose of bovine cartilage is 200 mg per 25 pounds of body weight.

Perna

Perna canaliculus, the green-lipped mussel, is a shellfish that is a natural source of highly concentrated glycosamino-glycans (GAGS) including chondroitin, as well as a number of other nutrients, including complex proteins, amino acids, nucleic acids, naturally chelated minerals, and an inhibitor of prostaglandin synthesis that makes it effective as an anti-inflammatory supplement.

My first introduction to chondroprotective nutritional products was a product containing *Perna canaliculus.* A new client who had recently moved to our area asked whether I could locate a product containing perna that his previous veterinarian had prescribed for Lizzy, his older, arthritic Old English Sheepdog. He told me that he was opposed to long-term drug therapy for his pet and that the perna product worked like a miracle. Without it, Lizzy couldn't even get up, much less walk normally. The perna product was safe, devoid of side effects, and very effective in helping his dog walk. Without this product, he would have opted for euthanasia due to her poor quality of life. I ordered the product for him and used it on several other dogs with good results. Perna is inexpensive and readily accepted by most dogs.

A new product called Glyco-Flex Plus (VetriScience) combines the benefits of perna with glucosamine and methylsulfonylmethane (MSM).

Sea Cucumber

The sea cucumber *Cucumaria frondosa,* also known by the names "trepang" and "beche de mer," are marine animals related to urchins. These organisms are believed to inhibit harmful prostaglandins involved in causing pain and arthritis. They are also rich in nutrients needed by cartilage, including chondroitin and mucopolysaccharides, and several vitamins and minerals. One popular product supplies the sea cucumber in a unique "jerky-type" treat that dogs find quite palatable. Other compounds found in this product include sea kelp, natural vitamin E, lecithin, garlic, omega-3 fatty acids, and glucosamine hydrochloride. Each jerky treat provides 1,200 mg of chondroitin.

In research testing by an independent laboratory, the product showed excellent anti-inflammatory activity in rats in which inflammation was induced by injection; no side effects were seen. The anti-inflammatory response was superior to that of Rimadyl and phenylbutazone. This study also showed that the product had higher anti-inflammatory activity than a product made from perna mussels and a glucosamine/chondroitin supplement, indicating that this product might be preferred if a dog fails to respond to another supplement. Since the response to various supplements varies among patients, if one fails to provide relief, another should be tried. However, to my knowledge the product has not been evaluated in double-blind placebo-controlled studies in dogs with naturally occurring arthritis. Clinical reports from the veterinary community indicates high acceptance and effectiveness.

The recommended dosage for this unique product is one piece of jerky per day for a 60- to 70-pound dog.

While the active ingredient in the product was assumed to be chondroitin, further research showed that while the sea cucumber contains chondroitin, another substance called InflaStatin (now under research and development) is the active ingredient.

I find these treats perfect for the hard-to-medicate dog. While some supplements are flavored pills, some dogs will not eat anything in a pill form. Some dogs simply can't be medicated by their owners. This may be because the dog was never taught to take medications as a puppy and now will not allow the owner to give it a pill, or because the owner finds giving their dog pills each day a hassle. However, offering the dog a jerky treat is an easy way to allow the pet to receive the daily recommended dose of medication.

The jerky treats can also be used in conjunction with other similar pill supplements, as overdosing a pet on glucosamine or chondroitin is unlikely. Many owners will give their dogs their recommended amounts of daily pills but will also reward the dog with a jerky treat. I like the idea of giving pets with arthritis a daily treat that is good for them, as is the case with this jerky product.

Shark Cartilage

Researchers have reported a link between blood vessel growth and the development of arthritis. In the joint fluid of arthritic pets, there is an increasing amount of a chemical called endothelial cell-stimulating angiogenic factor. This chemical encourages growth of new blood vessels in the arthritic joint. It is theorized that by inhibiting new blood vessel growth, further degeneration of cartilage might be prevented.

In the laboratory, shark cartilage has been shown to contain chemicals that inhibit blood vessel formation. Because arthritis is an inflammatory condition, and inflammation requires blood vessels, it has been suggested that shark cartilage can benefit arthritic pets by inhibiting the formation of new blood vessels. And in fact, research has shown this to be the case. In studies in both people and in dogs, significant improvement is seen in patients suffering from arthritis. Arthritic pets and people taking shark cartilage supplements often experience increased mobility and decreased pain.

In one study, 8 of 10 dogs showed improvement when treated at a dosage of 750 mg per 5 kg of body weight for 3 weeks. Improvement was defined as no continuing lameness, lack of swelling and pain, and improved movement. When treatment was temporarily discontinued, pain and lameness returned. Administering additional shark cartilage at 50 percent of the original dose resulted in improvement. The relief from pain and inflammation was theorized to occur as a result of decreased blood vessel formation. Improvement may also result from a relief from pain due to the large amount of mucopolysaccharides contained in the cartilage, which can help nourish and heal the cartilage. As a result of studies such as this one, many veterinarians feel it prudent to prescribe shark cartilage, as the supplement can be beneficial in some pets with arthritis and can substitute for therapy with medications like NSAIDs that have potential side effects.

> Arthritic pets and people taking shark cartilage supplements often experience increased mobility and decreased pain.

The main problem with using shark cartilage to treat arthritis is the large dosage required (750mg/5kg). This suggested dosage would require giving a large number of capsules to the pet each day. Since shark cartilage is among our more expensive supplements (approximately $40 to $50 for a 2-week supply for a large dog), the dosage of shark cartilage needed for medium- to large-breed arthritic dogs is unaffordable for most pet owners.

Several products on the market supply a much lower dosage of shark cartilage than that listed in the studies reported to date. This lower dosage has proved beneficial in some arthritic dogs. Because shark cartilage is very expensive to use in larger dogs, owners are often tempted to give less than the recommended dosage to decrease cost. This lower dosage can be acceptable after a 1- to 2-month stabilization period. Work with your doctor to determine the most effective dose for your dog. As is often the case with supplements, we don't know the best or most effective dose for shark cartilage. We must therefore use the products currently available and adapt the dosage to the individual pet's needs.

Glucosamine and Chondroitin Sulfate

Glucosamine is the most commonly used chondroprotective supplement used for the treatment of osteoarthritis. Chondroitin is the second most commonly used supplement for the treatment of osteoarthritis. Glucosamine is an aminosugar that is incorporated into joint cartilage. It is supplied as a supplement in one of three forms: glucosamine sulfate, glucosamine hydrochloride, or N-acetylglucosamine. Studies show that while all three forms of glucosamine are effective, glucosamine hydrochloride and glucosamine sulfate were more effective than N-acetylglucosamine. Glucosamine is rapidly taken up by cartilage cells and helps stimulate the synthesis of joint fluid and cartilage and also helps inhibit the destructive enzymes that can destroy cartilage and pro-teoglycans. The anti-inflammatory aspect of glucosamine may result from the scavenging of harmful free radicals simi-lar to antioxidants. Glucosamine is used by the cartilage for the synthesis of glycosaminoglycans.

A number of studies in people and pets show that glu-cosamine is equally effective for treating osteoarthritis when compared to NSAIDs, and without the side effects.

While a number of glucosamine products are available from reputable manufacturers, many of the early major stud-ies done in pets have used a proprietary product (Cosequin and Cosequin-DS) containing glucosamine and chondroitin. Clinical evidence indicates other products from well-known manufacturers are also effective.

Glucosamine is very safe with no side effects. Mild GI upset is rarely observed.

Dosages vary depending upon the product. As a guide-line for combination products, a starting dose of 1,000 to 1,500 mg of glucosamine with 800 to 1,200 mg of chon-droitin is recommended per day for a 50- to 100-pound dog. This dose is then lowered after 4 to 8 weeks.

Chondroitin sulfate is the major glycosaminoglycan found in cartilage. It also helps slow down enzymes that are destructive to the joint. A study in the 1998 journal *Osteo-arthritis and Cartilage* (as referenced in *The Natural Phar-macy: Arthritis,* Hobbs and Bucco, Prima,1999) reported that chondroitin sulfate is an effective treatment for osteo-arthritis. Because chondroitin production decreases with age, supplements with this compound may be especially helpful for older pets with arthritis.

Chondroitin is often added to supplements containing glucosamine. While significant studies are lacking, many people feel that adding chondroitin to glucosamine enhances the ability of both substances to repair cartilage.

The trace element manganese is necessary for the synthesis of proteoglycans and serves as an antioxidant. The biochemical reactions that make glycosaminoglycans from glucosamine will not occur efficiently unless manganese is present in the body. An estimated 37 percent of American people may be marginally deficient in manganese, which limits the rate of glycosaminoglycan (GAG) synthesis. One particular glucosamine-chondroitin supplement includes manganese to help ensure that GAG synthesis occurs at the maximum possible rate. Whether or not animals have manganese deficiency is not known so whether manganese supplementation is necessary for animals is unknown as well. Still, including manganese with this supplement will ensure the proper amount of manganese is present for the maximum rate of glycosaminoglycan synthesis, if it is needed.

> Because chondroitin production by the body decreases with aging, supplementation with this compound may be especially helpful for older pets with arthritis.

Glucosamine supplements are available in oral form or as an injection.

Using Chondroprotective Supplements

The following points are important to maximize success when using these chondroprotective supplements:

Safe and effective. They are extremely safe and equally effective when compared to NSAIDs.

A CLOSER LOOK

I've already talked at length about glucosamine and chondroitin, which constitute the major GAGS in the joint cartilage. Remember that glycosaminoglycans serve as a major component of articular cartilage.

Glycosaminoglycans function by decreasing the presence of harmful pro-inflammatory prostaglandins and other inflammatory enzymes that degrade the cartilage matrix. This results in reduced pain and inflammation, decreased enzymatic destruction of the cartilage, and stimulation of anabolic (cartilage-building) pathways. The GAGS also appear to increase the synthesis of proteoglycans, hyaluronic acid (which acts as a joint lubricant), and collagen. One novel product called Adequan contains glycosaminoglycans (specifically hyaluronic acid, or HA) extracted from bovine cartilage and is available in an injectable form (HA is not well absorbed orally). The recommended regimen is a series of eight injections, two each week for 4 weeks. If the pet has responded favorably during the 4-week trial, we then give the pet an injection as needed (usually one injection every 1 to 12 months, varying from pet to pet). This injectable product can be used with oral chondroprotective supplements as well. The injectable product can be used to get a faster response than the oral supplements. Further injections are given as needed, or pets can be maintained on oral supplements according to the response seen and the convenience for the pet owner. *Note:* This product has also shown effectiveness when flushed into joints during joint surgery, allowing faster and smoother recovery (*JAHVMA,* August–October 1996). Side effects with GAGS are extremely rare, though dose-dependent inhibition of blood clotting has been reported. If you are concerned, have your dog's doctor regularly monitor blood coagulation parameters.

Less costly than NSAIDs. Cost may be an issue for some pet owners. The typical daily cost of using a glucosamine-chondroitin supplement is approximately $1.50 per day for a 50-pound dog. This cost can decrease as the dosage of the supplement is lowered to allow the owner to use the least amount of supplement to maintain pain relief. The comparable cost of the most popular NSAIDs is approximately $2 to $3 per day for a 50-pound dog, making these supplements less expensive, though they are equally effective and lack the potential serious side effects.

Most effective when used early. Since these supplements work by acting on living cartilage cells, they are most effective when used early in the course of the disease. This requires adequate and early diagnosis.

Response may take several weeks. That's because chondroprotective supplements are not drugs but rather nutritional supplements. During the first 4 to 8 weeks, an increased "induction" dose is used and then the dose is lowered as improvement is seen. Additional short-term therapy with conventional and complementary treatments can be used during the induction phase.

Can be effective prior to signs of disease. Supplements can also be effective when no clinical signs are present but disease exists. In my practice, many dogs are diagnosed with hip dysplasia via screening radiographs and started on the supplements pending the need for surgical correction or until clinical signs occur.

Purity of the products is important. Many generic products that sell for much less than patented products do not have the same quality. Studies that have shown the effectiveness of these compounds have used pure grades of products. Products of lesser purity, while they often cost less, may also be less effective. Unlike traditional drugs these compounds are not regulated, and labeling can be inaccurate or misleading. Manufacturers are not required to analyze their products regarding purity, uniformity, or content. Purchase only quality products from reputable manufacturers, as recommended by your doctor.

Reevaluate diagnosis if improvement isn't apparent. Because chondroprotective supplements are so effective in improving symptoms in arthritic pets after 4 to 8 weeks, the diagnosis should be reevaluated after this period of time if improvement is not seen.

Additional Supplements

Several additional items may be included in supplements.

Bromelain

Bromelain is an enzyme from pineapple that provides additional anti-inflammatory relief by stimulating the good protective prostaglandins and may be included in chondroprotective products.

Skullcap and Mullein

Skullcap and mullein are "natural" pain relievers that may be included in chondroprotective supplements. While not always necessary, including these agents may help make the pet more comfortable. This may prevent the need for additional conventional analgesics (pain killers).

Yucca

Pets with arthritis often respond well to supplementation with yucca, an anti-inflammatory that may be included in some

USING SUPPLEMENTS FOR DOGS WITH ARTHRITIS

Here's my general protocol for using supplements in dogs with arthritis:

- Make sure the pet is eating a good diet.
- Add natural vitamins and minerals to the diet. This forms the basis of all of our supplementation. Products I use include Canine Plus, Ligaplex, and Catalyn.
- Add omega-3 fatty acids in the form of fish oil (not flaxseed oil) to give anti-inflammatory relief.
- Use a supplement containing glucosamine and/or chondroitin.
- Depending upon the pet's response, I may add herbs, homeopathic remedies, acupuncture, and occasionally a non-steroidal medication for short-term use if needed.

products. Some doctors have reported that a point of tolerance may be reached in some patients where good results are no longer obtained. In the laboratory, the yucca plant contains chemicals that can be converted into steroids although it is not known if this also occurs in the body.

DMG

DMG stands for dimethylglycine. Low levels of it are found in foods including meats, seeds, and grains. Both the human and animal body make DMG from choline and betaine. Increased dietary intake of DMG has been suggested to be beneficial. The metabolic role of DMG is to provide carbon to cells. It is also a precursor of SAMe (see page 119).

DMG is extremely safe. The body converts it into metabolites that are either used or excreted from the body. It has been recommended for use in pets with a variety of conditions, including osteoarthritis, at a dose of 50 to 250 mg per day. Its mechanism in the treatment of osteoarthritis is via an anti-inflammatory effect. Research indicates that DMG reduces the incidence of arthritis and allows for the reversal of the inflammatory condition of some experimental animals with arthritis.

Many doctors prescribe DMG for horses, dogs, and cats to improve performance and enhance recovery from various health problems. DMG is considered an anti-stress nutrient. Studies have shown that DMG can improve the immune response by improving both cell-mediated and humoral (antibody) immunity.

MSM

Methylsulfonylmethane, or MSM for short, is a natural anti-inflammatory and analgesic. It is a stable metabolite of DMSO (dimethylsulfoxide). MSM supplies sulfur to the body, which can be used for the treatment of a variety of disorders including osteoarthritis, allergies, and digestive disorders. For example, sulfur is an essential chemical needed for the synthesis of cartilage, which may explain its use in the treatment of arthritis.

MSM is found naturally in a variety of foods including meat, fish, eggs, poultry, milk, and to a lesser amount, in vegetables, legumes, and fruits. Because of mineral depletion in soil and because MSM is lost during the storage and preparation of food, some concern exists that dietary sources may not provide enough sulfur to our pets. Additionally, the amount of MSM in the body decreases with age, indicating a possible need for this compound in older pets.

In arthritic cartilage, the concentration of sulfur is about one-third the level found in normal cartilage. MSM may help treat arthritis via an anti-inflammatory benefit and by providing sulfur used by the cartilage in the healing process.

> Animals with rheumatoid arthritis that were given MSM showed no cartilage degeneration.

Studies in people and animals showed improved joint flexibility, reduced stiffness and swelling, and reduced pain. Animals with rheumatoid arthritis that were given MSM showed no cartilage degeneration.

MSM is very safe and may help treat arthritis via an anti-inflammatory benefit and by providing sulfur used by the cartilage in the healing process.

MSM is considered very safe, although extreme over-doses can make animals ill. No long-term side effects were seen when human volunteers were given MSM for up to 6 months.

While MSM may be of benefit to pets, more research is needed to determine the optimum dosage and treatment schedule.

Cetyl Myristoleate

Cetyl myristoleate is an ester of a common fatty acid (myristoleic acid) commonly found in fish oils, dairy butter, and animal fat. It isn't clear how CM works, but it may act similarly to omega-3 fatty acids. Its effects, however, are often seen more quickly and last longer than when fatty acids supplements are used by themselves. Some doctors have proposed that CM can reprogram certain types of white blood cells (memory T-cells); others suggest that hyper-immune responses by the body are normalized and that CM may function as a joint lubricant as well as an anti-inflammatory.

Cetyl myristoleate can be combined with glucosamine supplements for greater results.

A major multi-center study involving people with rheumatoid arthritis showed significant improvement in 63.3 percent of patients using CM alone with 87 percent improvement in patients using CM and glucosamine. No adverse reactions were seen except for mild GI symptoms in five patients (the same signs were seen in three patients receiving a placebo). Veterinarians using a product called Myristin in combination with Myrist-Aid, which contains glucosamine, MSM, and other herbs and antioxidants, have reported success in dogs with osteoarthritis.

It appears that CM may be quite successful for treating many pets with arthritis without side effects, but more studies are needed.

SAMe

SAMe stands for S-adenosylmethionine. It is closely related to the ATP molecule that the body uses for energy for the cells. When ATP combines with the amino acid methionine, S-adenosylmethionine is formed. While it has been used in people as an anti-depressant, SAMe has also come under scrutiny as a possible anti-arthritic supplement.

In people, the result of one double-blind placebo-controlled study showed that SAMe was more effective at relieving pain than the placebo and as effective as the NSAID naproxen.

In this study, naproxen worked faster than SAMe, which took 4 weeks to achieve effect. At the end of the study, both

CHONDROPROTECTIVE SUPPLEMENTS

Chondroprotective supplements are among those more commonly prescribed for pets suffering from arthritis. Inclusion in this table does not imply endorsement or recommendation, nor does exclusion indicate that a product is unacceptable. As new products are introduced regularly, your veterinarian can guide you in choosing the correct supplements for your pet.

COMMONLY USED CHONDROPROTECTIVE SUPPLEMENTS AND THEIR INGREDIENTS

Supplement	Components	Manufacturer
Acetylator		Vetri-Science
Arthri-Nu	glucosamine, vitamin E, selenium, copper, zinc, omega-3 fatty acids	VPL
Arthrose	glucosamine	King Pharmacy
Cani-Flex	glucosamine	Vet-A-Mix
Cartiflex	New Zealand green-lipped sea mussel (a source of glycosaminoglycans (chondroitin), omega-3 fatty acids, vitamins, and minerals)	VRx
Cartivet	shark cartilage	Biotherapies
Cosequin, Cosequin DS	glucosamine, chondroitin, manganese, vitamin D	Nutramax
DMG Vetri-Cine	dimethylglycine	Vetri-Science
Generation	chondroitin, methionine, manganese, vitamins, minerals	Vita-Flex

Supplement	Components	Manufacturer
Glucosamine Single Source	perna mussel, glucosamine (in Glycoflex-Plus)	Vetri-Science
Glucosamine Multi-Source		Vetri-Science
Glucosamine		Vetri-Science
Glycoflex		Vetri-Science
Glycoflex-Plus		Vetri-Science
Hi-Potency Joint Recovery	shark cartilage, bovine cartilage, glucosamine sulfate, glucosamine hydrochloride, boswellia, devil's claw, ginger root, white willow bark, cayenne	Dancing Paws
Joint Maintenance	shark cartilage, glucosamine hydrochloride, glucosamine sulfate, aloe vera, horsetail stems, ginger root powder, ginkgo biloba leaf, citrus peel	Dancing Paws
Joint Rescue	glucosamine, chondroitin, boswellin, curcumin, bromelain, vitamins, minerals	Ark Naturals
NutriFlex	glucosamine sulfate, bovine tracheal cartilage, boswellia, sea cucumber, ascorbic acid, curcumin, ginger, bromelain, yucca, calcium ascorbate, magnesium ascorbate, zinc, manganese, copper	Rx Vitamins for Pets
Prosamine	glucosamine, manganese, vitamins, minerals	Virbac
Syno-Flex	perna mussel	Vetri-Science
Ultra-Flex	chondroitin, manganese, methionine	Vitality Systems
Vetri-Shark	shark cartilage	Vetri-Science

treatments produced positive benefit. However, naproxen produced more side effects, namely gastrointestinal distress (a common side effect of potent NSAIDs such as naproxen).

Another similar study compared SAMe to the potent NSAID piroxicam, with similar results and positive effects for the SAMe.

Exactly how SAMe is effective when treating osteoarthritis is unclear, but some theories have been offered. SAMe does show anti-inflammatory and pain-relieving properties. Additionally, laboratory research in the test tube suggests that SAMe might work similar to glycosaminoglycans (such as glucosamine and chondroitin) by stimulating cartilage cells to produce more proteoglycans. This research suggests the possibility that SAMe might help heal the joints as well as relieve pain and inflammation. In one study in rabbits, in which surgery was performed on the joint in an attempt to cause arthritis, SAMe-treated rabbits showed protection against the development of arthritis when compared to control animals. The treated rabbits had thicker cartilage, more joint cartilage cells, and higher proteoglycan levels.

SAMe shows anti-inflammatory and pain-relieving properties, protects the stomach lining, and may improve the mood of pets with arthritis.

While SAMe shows promise as a treatment for ostearthritis, it does not appear effective for other forms of arthritis, such as rheumatoid arthritis. SAMe also has some positive side effects in people. It appears effective as an antidepressant (and is used in people for this reason), protects the lining of the stomach, and protects the liver against various toxins. Current evidence suggests the toxicity is as close to zero as possible, making SAMe much safer than any drug currently used to treat arthritis.

Unfortunately, there is scant information about whether SAMe is beneficial in dogs. The recommended human dosages range from 600 to 1,600 mg per day, but there are no published veterinary doses as of this writing. Additionally, the cost of SAMe is quite high (several hundred dollars each month for the typical human dose). Although SAMe remains a possible supplement for use in pets, more research is needed, and the cost is prohibitive for most owners at this time.

CHAPTER SUMMARY

- Just as with conventional therapies, a proper diagnosis must be made before using complementary treatments on the dog with osteoarthritis.

- Supplements include nutritional supplements such as natural vitamins and minerals, chondroprotective or cartilage protective products, raw foods, and herbs.

- Supplements can be used with other conventional treatments or complementary therapies.

·6·

Additional Complementary Therapies

HERBAL TREATMENTS

HERBS PRESCRIBED FOR pets may be the whole herb or just the active ingredient in the herb. Products vary in terms of whether or not the whole herb or just a part of the herb is included. By using only the active ingredient, the other parts of the herbs (toxins, other ingredients that may make the active ingredient less effective) are not included. However, by using only the active ingredient, some of the other ingredients that might act in conjunction with the active ingredient are lost. Which way is better is up for debate.

A number of companies make herbs for the human and pet market, and standard quality controls such as those that exist for pharmaceuticals are lacking in the supplement market. Studies have shown that some products have more or less (and sometimes even none!) of the active ingredient listed on the bottle. For this reason, use only products from high-quality, reputable companies. In my practice, I use only herbs from companies with whose quality control I feel most comfortable. The least expensive generic supplements are likely to be of lowest quality and questionable value.

Herbs are usually supplied in powder, capsule, or tincture form. Many products made for humans can be used in pets. Unfortunately, the correct dosage for the pet has not been determined for many herbs; clinical experience and extrapolation from human data is often used. The following guidelines serve as a starting point for herbal therapy:

Western Herbs
One 500-mg capsule per 25 pounds, given 2 to 3 times daily

0.5 to 1.5 teaspoons of powder per 25 pounds, given 2 to 3 times daily

5 to 10 drops per 10 pounds, given 2 to 3 times daily

Chinese Herbs
One gram concentrated herbs per 20 pounds, given 2 to 3 times daily

4 grams fresh herbs per 20 pounds, given 2 to 3 times daily

Alternatively, some herbalists suggest using the recommended dosage for people and adapting it for the pet. Most human dosages are based on an "average" adult weight of 150 pounds. So if 5 capsules per day are recommended for a 150-pound person, a 30-pound dog would receive one-fifth of that or 1 capsule.

A variety of herbs are available for treating the dog with osteoarthritis. The study of herbal therapy can be divided into Western Herbal Therapy and Traditional Chinese Medicine (TCM). Similar (and often the same) herbs are used by both schools. The main differences between the Western approach and TCM include these factors:

Diagnosis. With Western Herbal Therapy, a conventional diagnosis is made (for example, your doctor would diagnose osteoarthritis). With TCM, a diagnosis typical of the Eastern philosophy might be made (for example, the pet with arthritis might be diagnosed as having a Wandering Bi syndrome that might exhibit the need for strengthening of the kidney yang). It is not too important which diagnosis is made, as the herbal therapy would be similar. The important point is that the proper diagnosis is made by the doctor before beginning therapy.

Herbs used. Another difference is the herbs used in each approach. With the Western philosophy, herbs such as willow bark or devil's claw might be recommended. With TCM, a combination of herbs with Chinese names such as *du huo* or *tang kuei* might be prescribed, although in the United States the herbs have Western names as well. What name is used is not important as long as the correct herb or herbal combination is chosen.

While herbal therapy may be effective in pets with arthritis, more research is needed to find the "best" herb or herbal combination and the most useful dosages.

Unfortunately, few studies have been done on the use of herbs for treating arthritis in pets. Therefore, most of our information is extrapolated from human studies and clinical experience in pets. Since so many other complementary therapies are quite effective in treating osteoarthritis in pets, herbs are not used as frequently. Still, should you wish to use them for treating your dog, or hear about the use of herbs for various conditions in pets, it is important that you are familiar with what is known about the herb treatment of arthritic pets.

Alfalfa

Alfalfa contains many nutrients and is one of the best herbal therapies for osteoarthritis.

Boswellia

The boswellic acids in this herb are useful for their anti-inflammatory action. In two studies in people with rheumatoid arthritis, one study found benefit in those taking boswellia and another study found no benefit. The conclusion was that while boswellia might be helpful, more research is needed.

Capsaicin or Cayenne

Capsaicin is the chemical that produces the hot sensation in peppers. It is incorporated into topical creams that are quite popular with people because it has shown to be effective when rubbed onto sore joints. In people, the only side effect from topical application is the warm sensation felt when the cream is applied.

While it might be effective, capsaicin creams are unlikely to be of much use in pets due to the amount of hair covering the skin. Additionally, it is possible that the cream used for people might be too uncomfortable for pets. Finally, unless the medicated area is bandaged, it is unlikely that the cream would have much contact with the pet's skin as pets are likely to lick off the cream, especially if any burning sensation is associated with it.

Devil's Claw

Devil's claw is used as an analgesic and anti-inflammatory and is often recommended for treating arthritis. Compared with a placebo, devil's claw produced a statistically significant reduction in pain experienced by people with osteo-arthritis; animal studies, however, are lacking. The herb appears to be safe for short- and long-term use. Many doctors do not use it in patients with ulcers since it may irritate the stomach lining much like NSAID medications.

Feverfew
Feverfew is often recommended in people for its anti-inflammatory effects in the treatment of osteoarthritis and it might be of benefit for pets with osteoarthritis as well.

Ginger
Ginger dilates blood vessels and may increase blood circulation to the arthritic joints.

Horsetail
Horsetail contains silicon which serves as the matrix in connective tissue development.

Licorice
Licorice is a fast-acting anti-inflammatory agent. Many herbalists regard it as "nature's cortisone" and often recommend it for pets with arthritis.

White Willow Bark
White willow bark was the original source of aspirin. Willow bark contains salicin, a component that was chemically modified to salicylic acid, which is common aspirin. It is used for pain relief and anti-inflammatory action. For people, the tea seems more effective than the powdered herb. Salicin is also converted by the body to salicylic acid, which means that the side effects of chemically produced aspirin could occur with willow bark. However, a very large amount of the herb is

COMMON CHINESE HERB FORMULAS

According to TCM, there is no one such entity as "osteoarthritis." Instead the TCM formula looks for deficiencies or excesses in various body systems. For example, one type of arthritis may exhibit dampness and wind, another might exhibit numbness, and yet another might need tonification of the Yin. This means that if using the Western diagnosis of "osteoarthritis," your pet's doctor might try several herbal formulas before finding which one works best. A variety of herbal formulas are available for treating pets with arthritis. The ingredients in each formula vary because of the Chinese diagnosis and classification of arthritis. Here are some of the common formulas and the desired result.

Eucommia: Strengthens the back and acts as a kidney yang tonic.

Rehmannia: Nourishes the liver and kidney.

Tang Kuei: Nourishes the blood and dispels pain.

Tuhuo Angelica: Nourishes the kidney yang and bladder to expel wind, cold, pain, and dampness; it has anti-inflammatory and analgesic properties.

required to get the same dose of active ingredient. Salicin is slowly absorbed in the intestines. This means that it takes longer for relief to occur after taking willow bark, but that the effects are longer lasting than salicylic acid. (This herb, by the way, may be toxic in cats.)

Cinnamon Bark: Warms the circulation and acts as a spleen tonic.

Codonopsis: Warms the circulation and acts as a spleen tonic.

Ginger: Warms the circulation and acts as a spleen tonic.

Licorice: Harmonizes the body and nourishes the supporting structures (tendons and muscles) that can be involved in arthritis.

Hoelen: Drains dampness and acts as a spleen tonic.

Clematis: Relieves pain caused by wind and dampness and relaxes muscles and tendons.

Gentiana: Clears dampness and heat.

Deer Antler: Tonifies yang and warms and strengthens the bones.

Astragalus: Tonifies the Qi.

Epimedium: Acts as a liver and kidney tonic.

White Peony: Has analgesic and anti-inflammatory properties and relieves muscle spasms and cramps.

Using Herbal Treatments

Obviously, many herbal preparations on the market are quite popular with pet owners. Anecdotally these herbs may help pets, and there is certainly evidence that herbal therapies can help people with arthritis. Herbs have long been used in Chinese medicine, indicating the presence of positive results.

Finding good controlled studies for using herbs in pets is difficult since the funding is lacking when compared to what's available to pharmaceutical companies. One recent study compared a combination of Western herbs (devil's claw, yucca, and white willow in a base of alfalfa, watercress, parsley, kelp, and fenugreek), traditional Chinese herbs (white peony root, licorice, epimedium, oyster shell, lucid ganoderma, isatidis, corydalis), aspirin, and a placebo in the treatment of dogs with osteoarthritis. Results of the study showed that dogs treated with aspirin showed the most improvement. Therapy with the Chinese herbs, while not consistent, were better than placebo. In addition, the authors suggested that a higher rate of improvement might have occurred if Traditional Chinese Medicine ideas had been used to diagnose the animal, rather than Western diagnostics. The Western herbs were no more effective than placebo. In this study at least, the NSAID was most effective, the Chinese herbs were next most effective, and the Western herbs were ineffective.

> Herbs have long been used in Chinese medicine, indicating the presence of positive results.

This does not mean that herbs are of no use in treating pets with osteoarthritis. My conclusion is that more studies are needed to determine which herbs or combination of herbs might be effective for pets with arthritis. In my own practice, I prefer chondroprotective supplements as a first-line treatment for arthritis. However, I will use combinations of herbs if the dog requires multiple therapies due to severe arthritis or if the owner prefers herbs. This is supported by Michael Murray, M.D., author of a well-known book of herbal medicine for people, *The Healing Power of Herbs* (Prima, 1995). Dr. Murray recommends glucosamine compounds due to their over-whelming effectiveness in most patients. The only herbs he currently recommends for his human patients are a capsaicin cream or a combination of bromelain and curcumin to relieve inflammation.

With the use of any of these supplements for the treatment of arthritis, do not expect overnight results. I usually tell owners

> Keep in mind that often several different types of herbs can be used simultaneously in an effort to maximize the chance of a successful outcome.

to give the product at least 2 months to see whether it is effective. Usually, the products are used at an induction dose (often double the maintenance dose) for 4 to 6 weeks, then the dose is lowered to the maintenance dose once results are seen. Some of these products are expensive, especially for larger dogs. Once results are seen, the products are weaned to the lowest effective dose in order to decrease the costs to the owner. While we're waiting to see whether we get positive results, the pet may need another form of therapy to give immediate pain relief and control inflammation. Acupuncture, homeopathy, and even short-term use of corticosteroids or non-steroidal anti-inflammatory medications may be helpful.

Occasionally, despite considerable improvement, some dogs experience a particularly "bad" day, even when supplements including herbs are generally working. Medical therapy or acupuncture or homeopathy can be useful during these "bad" days.

Keep in mind that often several different types of herbs can be used simultaneously in an effort to maximize the chance of a successful outcome. Using multiple products may also decrease the need for conventional therapies. Work with your pet's doctor to determine which course of therapy is best for your pet.

After reviewing all these supplements, you may still wonder which ones you should use for your pet. You and your veterinarian will have to determine this on the basis of your pet's individual needs.

ACUPUNCTURE

ACUPUNCTURE IS AN excellent complementary therapy to relieve the pain and inflammation associated with arthritis. Most dogs tolerate acupuncture well with no signs of discomfort; many actually relax or fall asleep during treatment.

I usually combine acupuncture with supplements designed to heal the cartilage, as acupuncture will not do this. Once the pet has improved, I use acupuncture only when the pet shows increased stiffness.

Traditional acupuncture involves the placement of tiny needles into various parts of a pet's body. These needles stimulate acupuncture points that stop the signs of arthritis. After acupuncture in its purest form, the dog stops limping. Other forms of acupuncture involve laser therapy; aquapuncture, when tiny amounts of vitamins are injected at the acupuncture site for a more prolonged effect; and electroacupuncture, when a small amount of non-painful electricity stimulates the acupuncture site for a more intense effect.

In traditional acupuncture, the acupuncturist places tiny needles at various points on the pet's body. These points are chosen based on diagnostic tests or traditional formulas. These acupuncture points correspond to areas of the body that contain nerves and blood vessels. By stimulating these points, acupuncture is theorized to stimulate the release of various chemicals, called endorphins and enkephalins, in the body. These chemicals, through inhibition of pain, stimulation of the immune system, and alterations in blood vessels, cause a decrease in the clinical signs.

As a rule, acupuncture compares quite favorably with other options for the treatment of arthritis. In some cases, acupuncture may be preferred when conventional therapy is ineffective or potentially harmful (such as long-term therapy for pain relief with corticosteroid drugs). Other times, acupuncture may be used when an owner cannot afford conventional treatments (such as back surgery for intervertebral disk disease or hip replacement surgery for the pet with severe hip dysplasia). The holistic ideal is that the owner and the doctor discuss both acupuncture and conventional therapies to allow the owner to make the best decision for the dog.

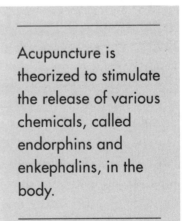

Acupuncture is theorized to stimulate the release of various chemicals, called endorphins and enkephalins, in the body.

Side effects from acupuncture are rare. Accidental puncture of a vital organ can occur. Infection can occur at the site of needle insertion. On very rare occasions, the needle can break and surgery may be needed to remove it.

Some pets require sedation in order to allow insertion of the acupuncture needles. In some animals, signs may worsen for a few days before they improve.

Many owners worry that acupuncture is painful and that their pets will suffer. Usually acupuncture is not painful. Occasionally, the animal will experience some sensation as the needle passes through the skin. Once the needles are in place, most animals will relax and some may become sleepy. Fractious animals may require mild sedation for treatment.

The number of acupuncture treatments that a pet will require varies from pet to pet. Usually, owners are asked to commit to eight treatments over 2 to 3 weeks to assess whether acupuncture will work. On average, treatments last about 15 to 30 minutes for needle acupuncture, and 5 to 10 minutes for aquapuncture or electroacupuncture. If the pet improves, acupuncture is done "as needed" to control the pet's signs.

Here is an example of a case from my practice where acupuncture worked wonderfully for a pet with arthritis secondary to hip dysplasia. Dusty, a 3-year-old Shetland Sheepdog (Sheltie) was lame. Radiographs taken while Dusty was sedated revealed severe hip dysplasia of both hips. Additionally, the hips were easily dislocated while Dusty was sedated. The owner wanted a total hip replacement performed, but the surgeon said that Dusty was too small for this procedure because the implants are only made for medium- to large-size dogs. The owner considered other surgical options, but did not proceed with those. We started Dusty on supplements including glucosamine, fatty acids, and chondroitin, and began acupuncture treatments twice weekly. After 4 weeks, we switched from traditional needle acupuncture to electroacupuncture. After eight treatments, Dusty was doing quite well. The owner has maintained

Dusty only on supplements, with the instructions to return as needed for further acupuncture.

Acupuncture points that work well for dogs with hip dysplasia include GB-29, GB-30, and BL-54. Usually, these are the only three points I use. Other points can be selected if the pet does not respond to this particular regimen.

As you can tell, it's vitally important that a correct diagnosis be made *before* acupuncture is attempted. Many owners seem surprised that I stress careful diagnosis, and seem to prefer that I simply grab some needles and start treatment! However, I must first answer these questions: Where do I place the needles? Will acupuncture help this pet? I can't answer these questions without a proper diagnosis. Regardless of whether an owner wants conventional treatment, alternative treatment, or a combination of both, we *must* have a correct diagnosis. This is yet another good reason to make sure the person performing acupuncture is a veterinarian. Only veterinarians can make a proper diagnosis and prescribe the correct course of therapy.

MAGNETIC THERAPY

IN RECENT YEARS, therapy using magnets has gained a following among some doctors and pet owners. It is seen as a safe, simple method of treating various disorders, often producing positive results without side effects or much expense. Does magnetic therapy really work? And if so, might your dog benefit from magnetic field therapy?

Magnetic therapy is by no means "quackish." The Earth has a normal magnetic field. The cells in our bodies and pets' bodies also have a normal magnetic field that allow for proper functioning. NASA determined that rats not provided with a suitable magnetic field in space perished due to disrupted energy flow from altered calcium metabolism. Some doctors attribute many common illnesses to the decline over the centuries in the Earth's normal magnetic field.

Doctors theorize that magnets work by means of magnetic lines of force; the strength of the magnetic field is measured in units called gauss. The higher the gauss number, the stronger the magnet. For example, a 1,000-gauss magnet is stronger than a 100-gauss magnet. Magnets are used either as permanent magnets, also called static magnets, or as pulsed electromagnetic field magnets (PEMF). Static magnets come in bars, beads, or strips. PEMF uses pulsing current flow through a wire coil to create a magnetic field around the wire: the greater the amount of current flow, and the greater the number of turns of the wire, the greater the magnetic field that forms. In people, the FDA has approved PEMF for treating nonunion fracture, fractures that have failed to heal. Other uses include avascular necrosis of the hip, osteoarthritis, and rotator cuff injuries. No toxic effects have been reported using magnetic therapy.

Magnets increase blood flow to the area, bring in essential nutrients, and help relieve pain and inflammation. Magnets appear to heal the body by removing inflammation and restoring circulation. By increasing blood flow to a diseased site, increased nutrients are available for healing. In fracture healing, for example, the use of magnetic fields increases the adherence of calcium ions to the blood clot formed at the site of the break. This allows proper formation of the callus that is necessary for fractures to heal properly.

In the Eastern view of healing, magnets help restore the energy flow of the body to allow healing and proper metabolism. This is similar to one of the theories used to explain the positive effects of acupuncture as well.

For your pet, magnets may be useful as part of a holistic therapy approach for arthritis. They should not be used in acute infectious conditions, on cancerous growths (although some doctors do find them useful in treating cancerous tumors), in acute injuries, in pregnant animals, or in dogs with cardiac pacemakers.

In one study, Dr. Michael Strazza found a reduction of 40 to 50 percent in the healing time of simple fractures by incorporating magnets into the bandage. This meant that dogs would resume weight-bearing sooner if magnets were used along with conventional fracture repair. A problem often seen in fracture healing is non-union of the fracture. In a nonunion, the ends of the fracture fail to heal and the fractured ends of the bones remain. With treatment of over 50 fracture cases, no cases of nonunion developed. In two cases of severe nonunion referred for evaluation where the fracture had failed to heal, magnetic therapy allowed healing of the fracture site.

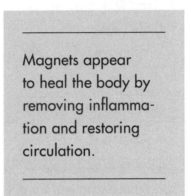

Magnets appear to heal the body by removing inflammation and restoring circulation.

Dr. Strazza also reports good success in treating various types of arthritis with magnets. Included in his cases are dogs with spinal arthritis and paralysis, chronic disk disease, hip dysplasia and arthritis, older dogs that move stiffly or slowly, and stiffness that develops after a morning exercise routine. By using a combination of a magnetic mat for sleeping along with a spinning magnetic field, he has achieved positive response in 60 to 70 percent of his cases.

For those pet owners who do not want to use a magnetic mat, magnetic collars are also available. The Magnatherapy collars use hematite crystals, which are by-products of iron ore. The collars are worn by the dog (or cat) and are reported to be safe and effective as an aid in the treatment of osteoarthritis.

> Magnets are certainly not a cure-all for every medical problem. Still, they are a safe and relatively inexpensive alternative for pets with chronic arthritis.

Magnets are certainly not a cure-all for every medical problem. Still, they are a safe and relatively inexpensive alternative for pets with chronic arthritis. Magnetic field therapy helps the body to heal by creating a favorable environment for repair. Since specialized magnets are needed for use in therapy, talk with your doctor about his recommendation for a source of the magnets if he feels this therapy might help your pet.

HOMEOPATHY

HOMEOPATHY, FIRST PROPOSED by Dr. Samuel Hahnemann in 1790, is based on the law of similars ("like cures like"). A substance that can create a transient set of symptoms in a healthy person will cure an ill animal or person that has the same pattern of symptoms. To select a matching remedy, a practitioner uses an index of symptoms to see what remedies are known to produce the symptoms shown by this animal now and in the past. He then reads about the remedies selected from his search in the *materia medica* (books that describe the symptoms found when testing the remedies) and chooses the one that most closely fits the animal's past and current characteristics. If we find the remedy that is similar to the patient, it reinforces the body in its direction of healing. The remedy does not change the symptoms, it pushes the body's own healing capacity to react to the remedy by curing the symptoms. If a joint is swollen and painful, there is an underlying problem in the energy field causing this. When the proper remedy is given, the inflammation will subside due to the efforts of the animal, not a drug.

How the remedies are made can sound strange to those hearing about homeopathy for the first time. As a doctor trained in conventional medicine, I too, was skeptical when I first heard about the concept of "like curing like" with super dilutions. Around 2,000 substances have been tested (proved) in a diluted form. Substances are diluted and shaken (succussed) so far that by a strength of 12C (1 part substance diluted in 99 parts water and repeated 12 times) there are no molecules of the original substance left in the homeopathic remedy. Yet as further dilutions and succussions are made (30C, 1000C, and more), the medicine becomes stronger and stronger.

While homeopathic remedies are generally considered safe when used correctly, the remedies of higher potencies have the potential to harm the pet. Therefore, without special training, no one should give over a 30C potency. In effect, it seems like all we're giving the pet is water and alcohol, which are the diluents for the original substance. Certainly pets can't get better drinking water and alcohol.

Yet many do get better. No, homeopathy is not 100 percent effective in every pet, but homeopathic treatment does work. The energetic pattern from the original substance imprints onto the diluent, so when a correct match is made, the energy pattern stimulates the body's energy pattern to heal.

Skeptics may claim it is a placebo effect. Certainly placebo effects are powerful in human medicine. You want to get better, you want the treatment to work, so it works. However, this placebo effect is all but impossible to reproduce or observe in pets. You can't tell your dog that the homeopathic remedy he's taking will make him stop walking with a limp, so he just decides to stop limping! Either the treatment works or it fails.

When I first started learning about homeopathy I thought it sounded too good to be true, and it certainly didn't make any sense from a scientific perspective. Yet after trying it a few times and seeing some impressive results, I became convinced that for some pets, homeopathy is a viable alternative, or addition to other approaches.

The most interesting thing about homeopathy is that, like other holistic modalities, it will make the dog healthier in many ways unrelated to the arthritis.

One nice thing about homeopathy is that it is virtually devoid of any side effects when prescribed carefully and correctly. If low potencies (6X, 6C, 12C, 12X) are given for a few weeks or when needed for a few days, even the remedy that is not the best choice can still help the animal and not cause harm. If high strengths (200C, 1M, 10M) are given too frequently, or if the wrong high-potency remedy is given, they are powerful enough to cause new symptoms and even a worsen of the overall condition.

From what I have said so far, you can see that using a well-trained homeopathic veterinarian will give your pet the best chance of a cure with homeopathy. (The Academy of Veterinary Homeopathy has a referral list of certified veterinarians. www.theAVH.org.)

Is there any proof that homeopathy works? Of course, homeopathic practitioners would say that they are effective.

From my own experience, many of my clients swear that their own illnesses have been helped by homeopathic remedies prescribed by their doctors. I have seen a number of pets improve with homeopathy as well. However, as with any therapy, there are those cases for which no treatment is effective. Additionally, I rarely practice "classical homeopathy." With classical homeopathy, one remedy is used at a time. The animal's response is carefully evaluated—everything about the dog, not just the lameness—to determine the next remedy. Most of my patients are prescribed a number of therapies in addition to homeopathic remedies so it is impossible to say which particular therapy was effective. In many cases the positive effect is probably a result of the combination of treatments. If you choose to work with a homeopathic veterinarian, they have been trained to evaluate the response prompted by the remedy as well as the supplemental care given.

Are there scientific studies proving the effectiveness of homeopathic remedies? Some studies have shown positive effects in patients treated with homeopathic remedies when compared to placebos.

One study in England evaluated the response of people with rheumatoid arthritis to homeopathic treatment. 80 percent of the patients treated with individualized remedies improved where only 20 percent of the placebo treated patients improved (Gibson, 1980).

Another double-blind study showed that patients with hay fever who received homeopathic remedies required only half the dosage of antihistamines needed by patients taking placebos. Other studies showed no difference in patients taking homeopathic remedies when compared to patients taking placebos.

I feel that homeopathy may be helpful for some dogs but that more studies are needed.

COMMON
HOMEOPATHIC REMEDIES

Remember that remedies are chosen using all the problems and characteristics, so these are merely a few that a homeopathic veterinarian may choose to prescribe for an animal with arthritis.

Bryonia: For pets whose pain gets worse and worse as they move around. They are often very thirsty and the least touch pains them so they snarl or bite.

Rhus toxicodendron: These animals are very stiff when they get up, then move more easily as they exercise. (Like a rusty gate!) Too much exercise can make them stiff again. They are worse from cold and damp and can be very restless with trouble settling down.

Caulophyllum: The smaller joints (toes, wrist, ankle) are often affected in animals needing this remedy.

Hecla lava: Bony arthritic projections often form in and around joints. Hecla may prevent new bone deposits and even have the body dissolve the extra bone.

Pulsatilla: This may help when pains are better from cold applications and cold weather. Often the stiffness is in the rear legs, and like Rhus tox, the pains are the worst with first motion. These very friendly animals are often not very thirsty.

Calcarea carbonica: This is often need for overweight, injury prone dogs. The hips are often affected and are worse for cold, damp weather.

Using Homeopathy Safely

Because it can be so difficult to determine the best remedy (called the "simillimum"), a thorough examination, history, and laboratory tests must be performed by the homeopathic physician.

My only concern with homeopathy, as with many other holistic modalities, is that pet owners may decide to skip going to a veterinarian for a proper diagnosis and treatment and instead treat a pet with a serious or life-threatening problem with over-the-counter (OTC) homeopathic remedies. This would be an ineffective treatment and could result in further illness or even death.

By delaying proper treatment, owners who elect to treat with OTC remedies may do their pets more harm than good. Therefore, I recommend prompt and correct diagnosis and not relying on OTC remedies for all except the most minor clinical signs (such as mild itching or sneezing). If a pet with even minor signs does not improve in 2 to 3 days of treatment with an OTC remedy, the pet should be properly evaluated. Then the best approach would be to seek out a homeopathic veterinarian (see page 142). *Homeopathic Care for Cats and Dogs*, a new book by Don Hamilton, DVM, gives an excellent understanding of the principles and philosophy of homeopathy and even suggests a few remedies for arthritis. He does suggest that the best results are obtained by consulting a trained practitioner. Several reasons for not going to health food stores and trying any of these OTC remedies yourself include:

1. Many of the OTC remedies are combination potions rather than a single homeopathic remedy. It is preferable to find the one remedy at a time that most closely matches your pet's constitution and symptoms.

2. OTC remedies are the least dilute and least potent remedies that can be used to treat your pet. While lower potencies are not likely to be harmful, the more powerful prescription remedies available through your doctor are more likely to be effective.

3. Most importantly, all pets with lameness are not necessarily arthritic. Since serious diseases such as cancer and immune disorders can cause pets to become lame, failing to seek medical help and trying home remedies can be dangerous. While homeopathy can be helpful, you should only treat pets homeopathically under a trained homeopathic veterinarian's supervision.

I feel that homeopathy works better if the dog is also using nutritional supplements, a great diet, minimal vaccinations and adjuncts to help reduce inflammation and pain. I like my arthritic patients to be "nutritionally healthy" before we start homeopathy or any other complementary therapy. Making sure the dog has a good diet is the subject of the next chapter.

CHAPTER SUMMARY

- Acupuncture relieves the pain and the signs of osteoarthritis, but does not cure the disease.

- Magnetic therapy helps the body to heal by creating a favorable environment for repair.

- Homeopathy triggers the body's healing response with the help of dilute solutions.

· 7 ·

Diet and
Arthritis

ONE OF THE most important factors you can control
with regard to your pet's health is its diet. You and
you alone control what goes into the mouth of your pet.

While diet is not the major focus of this book, diet directly
affects your pets and the diseases they acquire, including arthritis. An even more thorough discussion can be found in the
Natural Health Bible for Pets, from Prima Publishing in 2001.

There are some important points to consider regarding
diet and the holistic approach to preventing and treating
arthritis. You should be concerned about the amount of food
your dog eats as well as the general quality and specific nutritional content of that food. Dog food is not all the same.
You have a choice about the type of food your pet eats. Your
choices fall into general categories of processed food or natural-style food. Natural-style foods can be packaged or homemade. No matter which type of diet you choose, it must
meet these five requirements:

1. The diet must contain the proper amount and balance of essential nutrients required by the pet.

2. The ingredients must be of high nutritional quality so that the animal can effectively digest, absorb, and utilize the dietary nutrients.
3. The diet should be palatable so that the dog will eat it.
4. The diet should contain no "fillers," such as animal or plant by-products. If by-products are present, as in the case of some prescription-type diets for sick pets, the diet should contain the least amount of by-products.
5. The diet should contain no artificial colors, flavors, chemical preservatives, or additives, when possible.

A PROPER DIET

PART OF THE holistic approach to pet care concerns proper diet. Obesity is a major health risk for pets (and pet owners as well!). Keeping your pet from becoming obese is a prevention technique that every dog owner should practice. If your dog is obese, you can practice supervised weight-control methods that will lead to a fit animal. More on obesity as an arthritis prevention can be found in chapter 9.

> You and you alone control what goes into the mouth of your pet.

Proper nutrition throughout a dog's life is important to help prevent disease and to heal ill pets, including those with arthritis. There are inherent problems with generic, low-cost pet foods. While premium foods are much better, nutrients can be lost during processing and giving your dog supplements may be advised. Homemade diets are probably the most nutritious, both for general use from puppyhood throughout adulthood, and as a weight-control method for the obese dog.

The main decision facing pet owners is deciding which kind of food to feed—a homemade diet or a packaged processed diet purchased from the doctor or store. If you decide to feed your dog a processed food, select one that is healthy and natural rather than one made of entirely processed foods, fillers, and additives. If you decide to prepare your pet's diet at home, as many holistic pet owners do, you will need to decide whether the food should be fed raw or cooked and prepare recipes that are nutritious for a dog.

> Homemade diets are probably the most nutritious, both for general use from puppyhood throughout adulthood, and as a weight-control method for the obese dog.

As you make your decision, ponder these questions:

- Are you feeding your dog a healthy diet, with natural nutritional supplements?
- Are you instead feeding whichever food was on sale at your local pet store or grocery store?
- Is there any difference between the various diets on the market?
- Are premium diets really worth their cost?

Just what constitutes the "best" or most appropriate diet is quite a controversial topic, and there are as many opinions as there are doctors. Let's explore this issue for a moment.

Many pet owners and doctors have very firm opinions when asked the above questions. Often the opinions are based more on emotion than on objective medical facts. And finding facts to support one view or the other can sometimes be difficult.

For a moment, put aside any preconceived prejudices you might have when it comes to this subject. To choose the most holistic approach, keep an open mind and objectively view the facts so you can form your own opinion at the end of our discussion Your decision will depend on your circumstances and your pet.

PACKAGED FOODS

LET'S TAKE A look at packaged, processed foods first. Then we'll talk about preparing homemade diets for those of you who prefer to feed your pets in this manner.

Processed dog foods have been around for 40 to 50 years. Prior to the introduction of processed foods, our pets ate what we ate (or the leftovers of what we ate). Many holistic pet owners feel that pets fared much better then. Some people go so far as to claim that arthritis is a disease of processed food, meaning that pets fed natural diets do not suffer from arthritis. While I disagree since I see pets eating good diets that are afflicted with arthritis, I do agree that diseases including arthritis would be less common if we fed our pets better diets.

Processed foods were introduced (like vitamin-mineral supplements) for two main reasons:

1. Convenience
2. Prevention/treatment of nutritional diseases

There is no question that it takes at least some time to properly prepare homemade diets. Simply opening a can or scooping a cup of food from a bag and feeding the pet is certainly convenient. Just as processed foods save people time when it comes to human food preparation, so too do processed pet diets make feeding the pet easy, allowing owners to save time.

Processed foods were also introduced to prevent and treat nutritional diseases. It takes a lot more than simply tossing the pet some scraps to give the pet a complete, balanced, and nutritional diet. Prior to our scientific understanding of nutrition, both people and pets suffered from diseases resulting from dietary imbalances. For example, people who didn't eat citrus fruits were diagnosed with scurvy as a result of vitamin C deficiency. Pets fed mainly meat developed nutritional osteodystrophy (nutritional secondary hyperparathyroidism) as a result of calcium deficiency. Cats fed only fish develop thiamine deficiency and steatitis, an inflammation of body fat. By learning about the nutritional needs of pets and formulating "balanced" diets, these nutritional problems could be avoided. While many of the nutritional diseases seen prior to the introduction of processed diets have all but been eliminated, there is no question that processed foods, specifically those loaded with by-products and chemicals, may actually be contributing to a whole new set of problems.

When I think of packaged foods, I think of three classifications of diets: the least expensive generic processed diets, the more expensive premium diets, and the most expensive natural-style diets.

Generic diets are the least expensive but also the least healthy for your pet. Manufacturers use the cheapest ingredients possible. These foods that contain ingredients such as animal and plant by-products. Generic diets also are more likely to contain numerous preservatives and additives. By reading the label (see guidelines in sidebar, "Read the Label"), you can easily discern how unhealthy these diets are for your pet. Most generic foods are not fed to pets in feeding trials, but rather meet arbitrary nutritional "standards." Owners should not consider these generic diets because health problems, due to nutritional deficiencies, may result.

Premium foods are available at many pet stores and veterinary hospitals. They usually have higher quality ingredients than the generic diets. However, you must read the labels on these foods. While these diets are far better than generic diets, many contain animal and plant products raised with chemicals and hormones. While some of these premium foods can be acceptable choices when properly combined with natural supplements, they are not my first choice if the more natural diets are available. For many brands, however, the only thing premium about them is the price. Reading the label will help you learn to tell which foods to avoid and which ones can be used to feed your pet. Read on for tips on what to look for on these labels.

> Because of this insistence on quality and natural health, natural-style diets are the best ones (many would argue the *only* prepared foods) to feed your pet if you choose not to prepare a homemade diet.

The natural-style diets are the most premium of foods. They contain nothing artificial—no artificial colors or flavors. They use natural preservatives rather than chemical preservatives. Instead of by-products, they use more expensive ingredients which, depending upon the brand, are raised organically without chemicals or hormones. Because of this insistence on quality and natural health, these diets are the best ones (many would argue the *only* prepared foods) to feed your pet if you choose not to prepare a homemade diet. Examples of these diets include Wysong, Solid Gold, and Innova. Since these natural diets are the most popular with owners seeking a holistic approach to raising pets and the most healthy for the pets, let's take a closer look at what makes these diets so good for your pet.

The natural-style diets differ from most other packaged diets in the following ways:

- Natural-style diets use only human-grade, high-quality ingredients. Other prepared diets may use by-products of foods processed for but declared "unfit" for use by humans (see the table on the next page for a greater discussion about what's in some processed foods).

- Natural-style diets use foods, especially grains, in their whole state rather than parts of the foods. For example, a natural diet will contain whole rice rather than rice flour.

- Natural-style diets use no artificial colors, additives, chemicals, or preservatives.

- Natural-style diets are formulated for optimum nutrition.

To appreciate the difference between these classes of packaged diets, pet owners must learn to read labels and understand the differences behind the ingredients as they are listed.

WHAT'S *Really* IN PET FOOD

(THE INFORMATION IN this section is adapted from copyrighted material on the Web site of the Animal Protection Institute, www.api4animals.com, and used with permission.)

Most consumers are unaware that the pet-food industry is an extension of the human food industry, also known as the agriculture industry. Pet food provides a place for slaughterhouse waste and grains considered "unfit for human consumption" to be turned into profit. This waste includes cow tongues, esophagi, and possibly diseased and cancerous meat. The "whole grains" used have had the starch removed and the oil extracted—usually by chemical processing—for vegetable oil, or they are the hulls and other remnants from the milling process. Some of the truly whole grains used may have been deemed unfit for human consumption because of mold, contaminants, or poor storage practices.

While many of the various brands of pet foods on the market are virtually the same, not all pet-food manufacturing companies use poor-quality and potentially dangerous ingredients. Those companies devoted to producing natural, holistic diets are more likely to use fresher, human-grade ingredients that are better for your pet.

The price of pet food is often a good indicator of quality. It would be impossible for a company that sells a generic brand of dog food at $9.95 for a 40-pound bag to use quality protein and grain in its food. The cost of purchasing quality ingredients would be much higher than the selling price.

There are both bad and good sources of ingredients in your pet's diet.

Protein

The proteins in processed foods come from a variety of sources. It's no wonder pet owners are confused when they read terms like chicken, chicken meal, and chicken by-product meal. Here is how these terms are defined by the AAFCO, the American Association of Feed Control Officials.

Chicken: The clean combination of flesh and skin, with or without the accompanying bone, derived from the parts or whole carcasses of chickens, exclusive of feather, heads, feet, and entrails.

Chicken Meal: The dry rendered product from a combination of flesh and skin, with or without accompanying bone, derived from the parts or whole carcasses of chickens, exclusive of feather, heads, feet, and entrails.

Chicken (or Poultry) By-Product Meal: Consists of the ground, rendered, clean parts of slaughtered chicken (or poultry) such as necks, feet, undeveloped eggs, intestines, exclusive of feathers, except in such amounts as occur in good rendering practices.

When animals are slaughtered, the choice cuts such as lean muscle tissue are trimmed away from the carcass for human consumption. Whatever remains of the carcass (bones, blood, pus, intestines, ligaments, and almost all the other parts not generally consumed by humans) is used in pet food. These other parts are known as "by-products" or other names on pet food labels. The labels list the ingredients as by-products, but do not provide a definition for these by-products listed.

Many of these by-products are indigestible and provide a poor source of nutrition for dogs. The amount of nutrition found in the by-products of the meat, poultry, and fishing industries vary from vat to vat of food.

Some holistic veterinarians claim that feeding slaughterhouse wastes to animals increases their risk of getting cancer and other degenerative diseases. While this remains to be proven, there is no doubt that feeding these by-products provides little nutrition and may actually cause various diseases.

Fat

If you have ever noticed a pungent odor when you open a new bag of pet food, you are smelling refined animal fat, kitchen grease, and other oils too rancid or deemed inedible for humans.

Restaurant grease has become a major component of feed-grade animal fat over the last 15 years. This grease is usually kept outside for weeks, exposed to extreme temperatures with no regard for its future use. Rendering companies pick up this rancid grease and mix the different types of fat together, stabilize them with powerful antioxidants to retard further spoilage, and then sell the blended products to pet food companies.

These fats are sprayed directly onto dried kibble or extruded pellets to make an otherwise bland or distasteful product palatable. The fat also acts as a binding agent to which manufacturers add other flavor enhancers as well. Pet-food scientists have discovered that animals love the taste of these sprayed fats.

Carbohydrates and Grain Products

The amount of grain products used in pet food has risen over the last decade. The availability of nutrients in grain products is dependent upon the digestibility of the grain. The amount and type of carbohydrate in pet food determines the amount of nutrient value the animal actually gets. Dogs can almost completely absorb carbohydrates from some grains while up to 20 percent of other grains can escape digestion. Carbohydrates that escape digestion are of little nutritional value due to bacteria in the colon that ferment carbohydrates. Some ingredients, such as peanut hulls, are used strictly for "filler" and have no nutritional value at all!

Many pet food companies use a technique called splitting to hide the fact that less nutritional products actually make up a greater part of the diet. For example, a pet food might list the following ingredients: Chicken, Ground Yellow Corn, and Corn Gluten Meal. These latter two ingredients are both corn-based products, basically the same ingredient. When components of the same whole ingredients are listed separately, such as Ground Yellow Corn and Corn Gluten Meal, it appears there is less corn than chicken, even though the combined weight of the corn ingredients outweigh the chicken.

Flavorings

Garlic and onion are flavorings often added to processed foods. In the case of natural-style diets, garlic is often added for its purported medicinal properties as an antibacterial, anticancer, immune-stimulating element. At the dosages listed, the concentration of garlic is unlikely to be toxic and may be helpful to the pet. Onions are potentially more toxic (especially for cats in which severe anemia could result). It is not recommended to add onions to the diets of either dogs or cats.

Additives and Preservatives

Owners who desire to feed their pets a natural, chemical-free diet should be concerned about additives and preservatives. Many additives are added to commercial pet foods to improve the stability, appearance, or odor of the food. Additives provide no nutritional value and are mainly used to appeal to owners. Since pets are mostly color-blind, a dog has no desire to eat a nugget of food based on color. However, the owner may prefer to feed the dog a brown piece of food rather than one that is red. Artificial coloring added to the food in no way influences the dog's choice of diet but rather appeals to the visual sense of the owner who must purchase and then feed the food. Additives also include emulsifiers to prevent water and fat from separating.

Antioxidants prevent fat from turning rancid and antimicrobials reduce spoilage. They are necessary ingredients in pet foods, but natural antioxidants like vitamin C and vitamin E are better than chemical products such as ethoxyquin (EQ), butylated hydroxyanisole (BHA), and butylated hydroxtoluene (BHT).

> Many additives are added to commercial pet foods to improve the stability, appearance, or odor of the food. Additives provide no nutritional value and are mainly used to appeal to owners.

How prevalent are synthetic additives in pet food? According to research by the Animal Protection Institute, two-thirds of pet foods contains preservatives added by the manufacturer. Of the remaining third, most includes ingredients already stabilized by synthetic preservatives. For example, premixed vitamin additives that must be added back to pet foods to replace the vitamins lost during the processing of the food can also contain preservatives. This means that your dog may actually eat food with a variety of preservatives that have been added at the rendering plant, the manufacturing plant, and in the supplemental vitamins.

ªA CLOSER LOOK

Adding chemicals to food originated thousands of years ago with spices, natural preservatives, and ripening agents. In the last 40 years, however, the number of food additives has greatly increased. Of the many recognized food additives today, no toxicity information is available for 46 percent of them. Cancer-causing agents are sometimes permitted if they are used at levels considered "safe." The risk of continued use of these cancer-causing agents has not been studied and the build up of these agents may be harmful.

Ethoxyquin (EQ), butylated hydroxyanisole (BHA,) and butylated hydroxtoluene (BHT) are the most commonly used antioxidants in processed food for animal consumption. While ethoxyquin use is worrisome among pet owners, 75 years of studies show the product appears to be safe when used at the low concentration of 0.015 percent. Additionally, ethoxyquin has been shown to interfere with cancer induction by other chemicals by binding carcinogenic chemicals and enzymes that convert harmless chemicals into those that can cause cancer. However, many holistic doctors claim that ethoxyquin is a major cause of disease, skin problems, and infertility in dogs.

Because many people fear using ethoxyquin, most of the better pet foods have stopped using it and have replaced it, as well as BHA and BHT, with natural antioxidants like vitamin C and vitamin E. While BHA and BHT are also approved for use in human and animal food at the recommended "safe" levels, most holistic pet owners also prefer to avoid processed foods containing these chemicals as well. These chemical preservatives are prevalent because they cost less than vitamin C and vitamin E. The less expensive generic diets are most likely to contain relatively inexpensive chemical preservatives. Once again, read the label if you choose to feed processed diets.

For the most healthy diet, you should choose a natural-style or homemade dog food that contains no additives. If you must feed your dog processed foods, look for one that contains the least amount of additives listed on the label.

Other Chemicals

Chemicals are present in processed dog food, just as chemicals are present in processed people food. Just as many people are realizing the effects these chemicals have in our bodies, holistic doctors realize that these chemicals have effects on dogs as well. Are any chemicals safe? Certainly, no one would argue that we have received many benefits from a wide variety of chemicals. However, when possible, it would be in the pet's best interest if non-chemical alternatives (natural antioxidants and preservatives) were used to minimize toxicity to the pet. A number of chronic disorders such as various cancers, immune diseases, arthritis, and allergies are blamed on the use of a number of chemicals contained in pet foods. Direct proof of this is lacking; in many chemical additives (such as ethoxyquin), years of use seem to suggest "safety."

> Foods with the lowest number of these chemicals, even those chemicals that are not known to be harmful, are most desired.

Lest you think all additives are bad or harmful, that is not true. Antioxidants must be added to pet foods to allow for a long shelf life. Ingredients such as emulsifiers help stabilize fats. Anti-caking chemicals keep the ingredients from binding together. The point of this discussion is to show which additives are included in pet foods. Foods with the lowest number of these chemicals, even those chemicals that are not known to be harmful, are most desired. Still, there is no doubt that even though these chemicals in the low amounts in pet foods are regarded as safe, we have no firm data to establish whether or not they may be related to many of these chronic disorders. Therefore, whenever possible, the healthier alternatives are to purchase the natural-style diets that do not contain these chemicals or to prepare healthy homemade recipes.

Keep the following points in mind when choosing food for your dog:

- A holistic approach includes a natural-style diet that contains fresh whole ingredients rather than by-products.

- Ingredients are usually listed on packaged food labels in descending order from highest concentration to lowest. The first ingredient makes up the largest amount by weight of the ingredients.

- A holistic approach includes a diet free of artificial colors, flavorings, and preservatives.

- A meat-based source of protein should be among the first two or three ingredients in the food.

Homemade Diets: Raw Versus Cooked and a Look at the BARF Diet

As an owner, you may have heard a lot or arguments for or against feeding your dog raw food versus cooked food. Many owners feel that feeding a raw diet is the only way to

READ THE LABEL!

Reading and understanding pet food labels is critical when choosing a packaged diet. Many pet owners tell me that the label of their brand of food says the food is "nutritionally complete," therefore it must be a good food. Here are a few tips on reading the labels on pet food.

- *Guaranteed Analysis.* This states the minimum levels of nutrients in the food. A food with a minimum level of 5 percent protein means that the food has at least 5 percent protein; it may have a lot more, possibly even too much! Also, there is no guarantee that this protein is a good-quality protein. Chicken feathers have at least 5 percent protein, but I promise you that your pet won't get any nutrients from this protein source!

- *Digestibility.* Poultry meal is a common protein source, but the digestibility of poultry meal varies from poor to excellent. Reputable manufacturers use higher quality ingredients; the quality of the ingredient is reflected in the cost of the food. Stay away from poorly digestible, cheaper generic brands.

- *Nutritional Adequacy.* Many products state that the food has been "formulated to meet the nutrition levels established by the AAFCO." Unfortunately, this just guarantees the food meets a mathematical minimum. Your pet may not be able to digest or absorb anything in it because the food never had to go through feeding trials to assess palatability, digestibility, and show whether the animals in the trials grew or showed signs of malnutrition. "Animal feeding tests using AAFCO procedures that substantiate that this food provides complete and balanced nutrition" means the food has been fed to pets and that no nutritional problems were detected. The better, more expensive brands use this designation after conducting costly feeding trials. However, read these labels carefully too. Just because the food passed feeding trials does not mean it does not contain chemical, additives, and fillers.

offer a truly healthy diet, and that cooking somehow destroys many of the ingredients in the diet.

Because this topic is so controversial and has so little science supporting many of the suggestions made on both sides of the topic, I would like to address key arguments made for and against feeding raw foods.

The BARF Diet

The argument over raw versus cooked pet food really concerns what has become known as the BARF diet, also called the Billinghurst diet after Dr. Ian Billinghurst, the doctor who came up with this concept. BARF is an acronym that stands for "Bones And Raw Food." In this diet, the pet is fed raw bones, raw meat, raw vegetables, and a carbohydrate source such as rice. The concept is simple: since the wild relatives of our pets eat raw meat, that is what our pets should eat. Let's take an objective look at many of the claims made by proponents of this diet.

CLAIM: *Our pets should eat what their wild ancestors ate.*

CONSIDERATION: While it is true that the wild ancestors eat raw, freshly killed foods, our pets are not wild animals but rather domestic relatives of wild animals. That doesn't mean we can't feed them a similar diet, only that we keep in mind that we are talking about totally different groups of animals with different lifestyles, exercise patterns, and health concerns.

CLAIM: *Raw meat is safe for our pets. Wild animals suffer no ill effects from raw meat.*

CONSIDERATION: Whether or not raw meat is safe is debatable, although most pet owners report no obvious health problems in pets fed raw meat. Conversely, many owners report healthier looking coats and skin, less itching, less arthritis, and general overall health improvement once pets are fed raw homemade diets. There are health concerns with feeding raw meat, including parasites and bacterial contamination. These are discussed at length further along in this section.

To say that wild animals suffer no ill effects from eating raw meat is ignorant and presupposes we know everything that happens to every wild animal. While most wild animals thrive on their diets (as would be expected), we also know that wild animals can become infected with parasites, which are transmitted to wild animal predator relatives of our pets, and that any infected meat could certainly cause illness in a wild animal. Unfortunately, I am not aware of any studies that have pursued this topic.

CLAIM: *Animals are more "acidic" compared to people. That is why they don't get sick eating raw meat.*

CONSIDERATION: I'm not sure what this statement means, or how someone could even measure a pet's "acidity." I assume that those who make this statement somehow assume that the "acid" in the pet's body in some way can detoxify anything bad in the diet. While it is true that wild animals have adapted to their diets, this in no way means that they are immune to problems associated with the diet. For example, if a wild animal were only able to eat the muscle meat on the prey, that animal would develop calcium deficiency as meat is low in calcium. If the meat were rancid and infected with bacteria, the animal could certainly develop food poisoning (as often happens with pets that get into and eat garbage). Meat infected with parasites can be eaten by animals and will result in the animal becoming infected with the parasite. So this statement concerning acidity just doesn't hold up.

CLAIM: *Raw meat is safe for our pets. Their systems are designed to handle any problems with meat.*

CONSIDERATION: This all depends what is meant by "safe." Certainly raw meat that was raised free of chemicals and hormones, and that isn't infected with bacteria or parasites, is safe. Owners who choose to feed raw meat must do all they can to ensure that this meat is "safe" and free from pesticide, chemical, and hormonal residues as well as parasite ova (eggs). Proper handling of the meat is needed to ensure that it stays "safe" at home (most food poisoning results from improper handling at home than from problems with the source of the meat itself).

When pet owners say that animals can handle problems with raw meat, I assume they mean that the digestive tracts and immune systems of our pets (and their wild relatives) can eliminate any infections or parasites before they cause problems for the animals. While it is true that a healthy pet is less likely to become ill, and that a healthy animal is less likely to develop disease when infected with parasites (although this depends upon the parasite and the number of parasites infecting the animal), raw meat can still make an animal sick. When following the guidelines listed below, however, this is highly unlikely and may be a risk you are willing to assume.

What I find interesting is the recommendation that it is acceptable to feed raw meat to pets except for raw pork or raw wild game (such as venison or rabbit). The reason for this warning (which I agree with, by the way) is that these meats are more likely to harbor parasites than beef or lamb. However, this warning seems contradictory. If our pets "can handle" raw meat because of their "acidity" and their immune systems, why couldn't they handle the parasites present in any raw meat? In the wild, animals eat raw pork, venison, and a whole host of other meats that proponents of raw diets caution should not be fed to our pets. To me this is an obvious discrepancy that discredits this argument about raw meat being safe for pets.

CLAIM: *Feeding dogs bones is safe.*

CONSIDERATION: Once again we need to define "safe." Most pets eating raw bones do not die, develop impactions of the digestive tract, or experience any health problems. Still some do, as most veterinarians will attest. Some proponents state that only cooked bones, which are softer than raw uncooked bones, are likely to splinter and cause problems. Once again, the choice about feeding any bones is left up to your discretion.

While it may seem that the evidence presented so far in this discussion suggests pets should not eat raw meat or bones, that is not necessarily the case. We have no real good studies comparing "health" of pets eating raw versus cooked foods, nor do we have any studies comparing the safety of either diet. From personal experience I can say that many of my clients feed their pets raw meat and bones and have not reported any problems in their pets. In fact, many feel that their pets are "healthier," have shinier coats, shed less, and have fewer health problems, such as itching and arthritis. Some proponents of raw diets suggest that health problems such as arthritis are problems of processed foods and are not seen in animals fed raw food. While I do not totally agree with this assessment, I do agree that eating the best diet combined with high-quality supplements can help pets maintain a healthier lifestyle when compared to pets eating highly processed foods containing by-products and chemical preservatives.

In the final analysis, the choice will be left up to you. Regardless of how you choose to feed your pet, it is important to properly supplement your pet's diet to prevent deficiencies and ensure maximum health.

For a complete discussion of nutritional and other supplements, see chapter 5.

Preparing a Homemade Diet

While holistic purists often recommend feeding a dog raw food, and while many of these doctors have not had problems with food poisoning as a result of their recommendations, you would be wise to be concerned about the possibility of infection from raw meat. The bacterium of immediate concern are *E. coli* and *salmonella*. Stories exist in the media about human illness and death from both of these organisms. E. coli seems to be of most concern from eating beef, whereas salmonella seems to occur mostly as a result of ingestion of poultry products (raw chicken, turkey, and eggs). Most homemade diets use beef or poultry as the main protein source; lamb, venison, or rabbit can be used, but I prefer to reserve these protein sources for pets that have medically confirmed food allergies. Pork, venison, and rabbit should definitely be cooked (and I would be inclined to cook *any* meat in a pet's

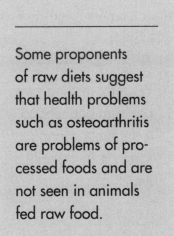

Some proponents of raw diets suggest that health problems such as osteoarthritis are problems of processed foods and are not seen in animals fed raw food.

diet). For owners who choose to feed raw meat, it would be wise to choose only animal meat that was raised "naturally" (without antibiotics or hormones), thoroughly wash the meat at home, and maybe even prepare the meat by grinding it at home (to prevent cross-contamination with other foods at the local grocery or butcher shop). Any signs of illness as a result of feeding raw meat diets should be evaluated by a veterinarian at once.

A better alternative is to feed the meat cooked (but not so well-done as to cook out all the nutrients) and the grains and vegetables raw or lightly cooked.

Dietary deficiencies (mainly vitamins and minerals) are more common with homemade diets. Careful attention to proper preparation is critical to prevent both deficiencies and excesses of vitamins and minerals. Natural, not synthetic, multivitamin and mineral preparations designed for puppies and adult dogs or adult cats should be used whenever possible. Some holistic practitioners also

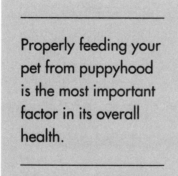

Properly feeding your pet from puppyhood is the most important factor in its overall health.

recommend the addition of colloidal minerals, which may be a better vehicle through which to deliver minerals to the pet. Child dosages (for puppies) and adult human dosages (for dogs) of human vitamin C and E preparations can also be added for their antioxidant effects. Calcium can be added in the form of bonemeal or calcium tablets (gluconate, carbonate, or the lactate forms are acceptable).

If you choose not to prepare a diet at home but prefer a commercially prepared diet that is close to natural, read the label to check for quality of ingredients (see sidebar on page 162, "Read the Label!") and lack of additives. Supplement with natural products such as brewer's yeast, fatty acids, kelp, barley grass, cooked liver, enzyme products, and sprouted beans or seeds. These natural supplements are often helpful to replace ingredients that may be lost during processing.

Properly feeding your pet from puppyhood is the most important factor in its overall health. The second important factor, exercise, is the subject of the next chapter.

CHAPTER SUMMARY

- Although diet alone cannot cure arthritis, it can help prevent the disease and ease the symptoms.

- Overly processed packaged foods are the least nutritious method of feeding your dog.

- Be aware of additives in processed packaged foods and read product labels carefully.

- Natural-style packaged foods, whether store-bought or from a veterinarian, are more nutritious.

- Homemade foods can be simple to make and are the most nutritious for your dog.

- There is no substitute for a healthy lifestyle as a holistic healing approach.

·8·

Exercise and Physical Therapy for Your Pet

THERE IS NO blanket answer concerning exercise and physical therapy for your arthritic pet. The best way to answer the question about how much the dog should exercise is enough to benefit his health but not so much as to further damage his joints or cause excess pain. The bottom line is that most arthritic pets can and should exercise. In addition to participating in good general exercise, arthritic dogs also benefit from specific physical therapy exercises designed to ease the pain and stiffness of their disease.

Dogs are dogs, and you certainly can't keep them in cages forever just to prevent further injury to damaged joints. Studies in people with osteoarthritis have found cardiovascular benefits and positive mental well-being provided by controlled physical exercise. The same is most likely true with arthritic pets.

EXERCISE

EXERCISE INCREASES MUSCLE tone, is good for the pet's cardiovascular system, strengthens the owner-animal bond, and encourages the well-being of the pet. Since muscles, tendons, and ligaments are so important in protecting the joint, maintaining strength and toning in these body parts is important. While various exercise regimens can be prescribed for human patients, most of these are impractical for pets. A moderate exercise program should be initiated under veterinary supervision. Start slowly and gradually allow your dog to do more as he progresses naturally on his own. If your dog can only go a half mile at a slow pace before experiencing pain, don't push him. Let your dog set the guidelines. The exercise should not lead to pain or discomfort. If your dog is sore the next day, skip that day and resume at a reduced pace.

For the severely affected pet, non-weight-bearing exercise such as forced swimming is ideal, as this strengthens the muscles, ligaments, and tendons while placing no force on the joint itself.

If you can swim your dog in a pool or tub while supporting his abdomen and chest with a towel sling, this is ideal. Of course, all dogs having access to a pool should be carefully supervised, as dogs can and do drown!

Strict rest, including cage confinement, is needed only when acute, painful flare-ups occur. During these days, your dog may benefit from acupuncture, or a dose or two of a non-steroidal medication. Massage or heat therapy, or both, is often beneficial on these days as well.

Regardless of which exercise you choose, simply commit yourself and do it! You may find that you, too, become more fit from exercising your pet, which is a nice benefit.

While we don't have the studies in veterinary medicine that prove the benefits of exercise for dogs as we have for people, clinical experience shows that pets that stay fit with exercise are healthier. And if we want to extrapolate from the human literature (as we are often forced to do), the studies are impressive. The January 1996 *Journal of the Ameri-*

can Geriatric Society showed that musculoskeletal injuries rarely occurred during exercise, and moderate intensity exercise did not exacerbate joint problems (as reported in *The Arthritis Solution*, Prima, 1997).

Another study in the *Journal of Arthritis and Rheumatology* showed that physical activity was associated with lower subjective ratings of pain than a sedentary lifestyle.

The good news is that a mild exercise program prescribed by your pet's veterinarian can be quite beneficial for your arthritic pet. Since each pet has unique needs and abilities when it comes to exercise, it is important to work with your doctor and communicate how your pet adapts to the prescribed program. The following cases will help illustrate this point.

> The good news is that a mild exercise program prescribed by your pet's veterinarian can be quite beneficial for your arthritic pet.

Pierre is a 2-year-old male yellow Labrador Retriever. Pierre was admitted to our hospital for neutering. Physical examination was normal prior to the surgical procedure. His owner reported no problems with Pierre that would indicate any underlying disorders.

Because all dogs, but especially a larger breed like Pierre, can develop skeletal problems such as hip dysplasia, we recommended testing Pierre for hip dysplasia while he was anesthetized for his neutering. His owner agreed with our recommendations even though she did not expect that Pierre would have any skeletal problems since he walked normally and loved to run, jump, and play, and never showed signs of discomfort or lameness.

After Pierre was anesthetized, I performed two procedures. First we laid Pierre on his back and extended his rear legs out and away from his body. This positioning allows us to get perfect pictures of both hip joints. Next, Pierre was rolled onto his right side. I then performed an orthopedic maneuver called an Ortolani maneuver. The Ortolani maneuver is performed by holding onto the thigh bone (femur) and pushing it towards the dog's spine. In normal dogs nothing happens, but in dogs with hip joint laxity (looseness) such as occurs in dogs with hip dysplasia, the femur pops out of the joint (resulting in a positive Ortolani sign). In Pierre's case, the right hip joint was normal (negative Ortolani sign). The procedure was then repeated on the left hip, which was also normal.

Pierre's radiographs were quite different; they showed severe hip dysplasia and severe secondary osteoarthritis on both hips, indicating chronic hip instability caused by hip dysplasia.

Occasionally dogs like Pierre have contradictory findings: the radiographs lead to one conclusion and the Ortolani findings show another conclusion. In these cases, read the worse signs. Since we do have opposite findings in some dogs, performing both radiographs and orthopedic maneuvers when evaluating dogs for hip dysplasia is important.

I reviewed the findings of hip dysplasia with Pierre's owner when she came in for his discharge from neutering. I discussed a number of options with her, including surgery to replace Pierre's badly damaged hips, medical therapy for pain if Pierre began to show signs of pain, and nutritional supplements to help heal the cartilage. Due to the high cost of hip joint replacement (approximately $2,500 per hip), this option was delayed while Pierre's owner budgeted for the procedure. She elected to correct Pierre's diet, replacing his store-bought food with a more natural processed diet. I also prescribed supplements for Pierre: omega-3 fatty acids and a product containing glucosamine and chondroitin.

Pierre's owner asked about exercising Pierre, since he enjoyed walks, chasing balls, and swimming in the neighborhood lake. Since Pierre was not showing any signs from his badly damaged hips, I told her exercise would be all right for Pierre. When possible, swimming would produce less stress on the joints. However, since the joints already had significant osteoarthritis, I did not think exercise could make things much worse for Pierre. If he showed discomfort during his exercising, his owner should cut back on those running and jumping activities that produced direct stress on the joints. Otherwise, I told her that Pierre, a very active young retriever, would be difficult to keep quiet and might develop behavioral problems (such as destroying the house and yard!) if he did not have an outlet (such as a controlled exercise program) to relieve this energy. At a recheck 6 months later, Pierre's owner reported that he was doing well and still showing no signs of pain or discomfort from his hip dysplasia and arthritis.

The owner of Bronwyn, another dog I diagnosed with hip dysplasia, was concerned about level of exercise. Unlike Pierre, Bronwyn occasionally experienced mild discomfort after exercising. According to her owner, this 2-year-old female boxer would from time to time be a bit sore after playing.

I sedated Bronwyn and took several radiographs of her hips and spine. The films showed very mild hip dysplasia without any evidence yet of secondary osteoarthritis. I also performed the Ortolani maneuver on both of her hip joints. Like the case with Pierre, her Ortolani tests were negative, indicating no evidence of laxity or dislocation in her joints.

As I do with many patients, I referred Bronwyn to an orthopedic specialist for evaluation. Under sedation the specialist performed a specialized procedure called a PennHip evaluation. This special test for hip dysplasia compares joint laxity as measured by a special instrument on the hip radiographs with a range of findings for the specific breed of dog being tested. In Bronwyn's case, the PennHip evaluation compared her joint laxity with that of other boxers. This evaluation showed that her hips were very mildly affected. Because of the large amount of thigh and hip muscling in the Boxer breed, and because of her normal PennHip evaluation, it is unlikely that Bronwyn would ever experience problems with her hips, unlike other less muscled breeds such as German Shepherds or Labrador Retrievers.

> Acupressure, massage, joint manipulation, and heat done at home are ideal forms of physical therapy that can help the arthritic pet.

In Bronwyn's case, surgery was not needed. Instead she, like Pierre, was placed on fatty acids and a supplement containing glucosamine and chondroitin.

Regarding her exercise regimen, her owner expressed concern since she wanted to use Bronwyn in dog shows and needed to train her for these shows. I suggested that she not push Bronwyn, but rather slowly adapt her to the regimen needed for show training. By slowly working up to the required level of exercise needed, Bronwyn could best adapt to the program. If Bronwyn was unable to work at this level due to hip pain, we would judge that based upon how she acted after her workouts and adjust things accordingly.

These two cases give a good overview of how important it is to evaluate each case individually and monitor the dog's level of exercise. Making blanket recommendations is difficult, as no one can predict the future. While it is true that extra stress on the joints will cause further damage, we must remember that "dogs will be dogs." We can't keep them totally confined 24 hours each day. Working with your veterinarian will allow you to find the best exercise regimen for your pet.

> Acupressure, massage, joint manipulation, and heat done at home are ideal forms of physical therapy that can help the arthritic pet.

PHYSICAL THERAPY

WHILE PHYSICAL THERAPY, such as performing stretching exercises, is limited in pets compared with people, you can still do things to assist your arthritic dog. Some physical therapy options must be performed by a trained professional; others you can perform on your dog at home.

Acupressure, massage, joint manipulation, and heat done at home are ideal forms of physical therapy that can help the arthritic pet.

Acupressure

You can be shown how to provide firm, sustained pressure to acupressure points to provide temporary relief of pain and inflammation from inflamed joints. I will often have the owners do this between acupuncture treatments.

Massage

Massaging the muscles of the affected limb can be quite helpful in reversing atrophy, or muscle wasting, that occurs in severely lame pets that have stopped using an arthritic limb. Muscle wasting is seen as early as 3 to 5 days after total disuse of a limb. Pets enjoy the gentle massage of the owner's hands, and the increased touching between pet and owner certainly increases that special human-animal bond. Muscles that are massaged daily, or several times each day, regain their tone and allow the pet to use the leg more quickly once the pain and inflammation of arthritis is reversed.

Manipulation

Manipulating the affected limbs allows the joint to be put through its normal range of motion. Severely affected pets not using their limbs have restricted range of motion. This allows scar tissue to build up and can result in permanent changes in severe cases. This is quite common in pets undergoing joint surgery as supervised manipulation is essential in preventing permanent "lock-up" of the limb. Your doctor can show you how to properly and gently manipulate the pet's affected limb.

Hot Packs

Providing warmth to the sore arthritic joint can bring temporary relief to your dog. Warm water bottles or heating pads can be used to provide 5 to 15 minutes of heat. Because electric heating pads can be dangerous and have resulted in severe burns in pets, it is essential that your veterinarian show you how to safely use the pads when treating your pet.

Laser Therapy

Low level laser therapy (LLLT) can be used to help pets with osteoarthritis. *Laser* means Light Amplification by Stimulated Emission of Radiation. The light from the laser is absorbed by chromophores (light-sensitive molecules in the cells) and is converted to chemical energy. Laser therapy has several effects, including increased cellular energy, reduced swelling, pain relief, muscle relaxation, and reduced inflammation.

The benefits of laser therapy for treating chronic arthritis in people and pets are comparable to those obtained with non-steroidal anti-inflammatory drug therapy without the side effects. In pets, lasers are usually directed at acupuncture/acupressure points. The pet can be treated at the doctor's office and in some instances an owner might be able to rent a small unit to use at home.

Electrical Stimulation

Electrical stimulation decreases pain and inflammation. It works by sending non-painful, non-harmful electrical signals that stimulate nerve endings, acting to decrease pain. Handheld units (called TENS units, for Transcutaneous Electrical Nerve Stimulation) can be purchased by owners who administer the treatment to acupuncture points designated by the veterinarian.

Ultrasound

Ultrasound uses sound waves to reduce inflammation by increasing heat and blood flow to the affected joint and surrounding tissues. The result is a warmed area soothing inflamed muscles. Although quite popular with people, ultrasound therapy is rarely used in pets, but could be a viable adjunctive treatment.

Exercise and physical therapy are important for pets with arthritis. Mild exercise, muscle massage, and joint manipulation will allow the pet to have some normalcy to his life and allow greater movement, keeping the joints functional as long as possible. By combining a good natural diet, necessary supplements, and an intelligent exercise program, you can help your pet live a comfortable life after the diagnosis of arthritis is made.

CHAPTER SUMMARY

- While few studies have been done on exercise and pets, studies in people with osteoarthritis show benefits to cardiovascular and mental well-being.

- Let the dog set the pace of its regular exercise program.

- Swimming is a good form of exercise for the arthritic dog.

- Physical therapy provides muscle tone that supports affected joints.

- Physical therapies you can perform on your dog at home include acupressure, massage, joint manipulation, and heat.

- Physical therapy methods that a professional can perform or train you to do include laser, electrical, and ultrasound treatments.

· 9 ·

Arthritis
Prevention

SOME TYPES OF arthritis can be prevented. Obesity, while not a direct cause of any type of arthritis, can contribute to the condition. You can prevent obesity in your dog by establishing good eating habits from puppyhood (see chapter 7). If your dog is obese, with or without a diagnosis of arthritis, various weight-control methods can provide your dog a healthier life.

Hip dysplasia is a common cause of osteoarthritis in older pets. An early diagnosis is key to keeping hip dysplasia from causing osteoarthritis.

OBESITY

OBESITY IS THE most common nutritional disease in pets. In both people and pets, it is a severe and debilitating illness. Because overweight arthritic dogs bear much greater additional stresses on already damaged joints, weight reduction is essential in these pets.

Estimates suggest that up to 45 percent of dogs and up to 13 percent of cats are obese. Personally I think these estimates are low, judging from the number of obese pets I see every day in practice. With rare exception, such as the presence of thyroid disease, obese pets are *made* that way, not born that way. Obesity is a disease of domestication. In the wild, few if any animals are obese. They eat to meet their calorie needs, and are always exercising when playing, fighting, and hunting for food. Ideally, you should work with your doctor from the time your dog is a young puppy so that you can prevent obesity.

Obesity Defined

How can you decide whether your pet fits the definition of "obese"? Current medical opinion states that a pet is obese when it weighs 15 percent or more over its ideal weight. Pets that weigh 1 to 14 percent over their ideal weight are considered "overweight" but not yet "obese."

While 15 percent does not seem like much, consider that a dog, such as a Labrador retriever (one of the most common breeds afflicted with arthritis) that weighs 69 pounds but should weigh 60 pounds is 15 percent overweight and is classified as obese!

An 11½-pound cat that should weigh 10 pounds is 15 percent over its ideal weight and would be classified as obese. As you can see, even just a few extra pounds on our pets is cause for concern.

Body Composition Score

While we often use weight to gauge obesity, I prefer to use a body composition score. Body composition more accurately reflects obesity than does a certain magical number. It also gives us something more concrete to shoot for, rather than arriving at some magic number. For example, while most people strive to achieve a certain numerical weight, a more accurate assessment would be to strive for a certain look.

While losing 10 pounds might be an admirable goal, being able to lose a few inches around the waist or fit into a smaller pair of pants is really the ultimate goal. I'm not suggesting you can't have a target weight when designing a weight-control program for your pet, only that this magic number is only a rough guideline of what your pet's "best" weight might be to treat obesity. I prefer to use the weight as a guideline but ultimately use the look and feel (measured by the body composition score) of the pet to know when we have reached our ultimate goal.

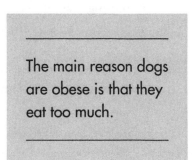

The main reason dogs are obese is that they eat too much.

The Cause of Obesity

Many theories about the cause of obesity are put forth by both doctors and pet owners; these include genetics, neutering, and disease. But the main reason dogs are obese is that they eat too much and don't get enough exercise.

Since female pets are more commonly obese than male pets, it has been suggested that hormones may play some role in fat retention and deposition. However, we really don't know nor do we have good evidence that gender has any primary role in obesity.

Since most pets are spayed or neutered, and therefore most obese pets are spayed or neutered, it is tempting to blame removal of the sex organs (and therefore sex hormones) as a cause for obesity. There is no hard and fast science to support spaying or neutering as a direct cause for weight problems in pets. Since spayed and neutered pets may be less active than intact pets, it may be that the inactivity (caused by removal of the sex hormones) contributes to obesity if the same amount of calories are fed. However, we have all seen spayed and neutered pets that are quite active. If you were to talk to any of my clients, few would agree that spaying or neutering has affected their pets' activity level. Although most *wish* the surgeries would calm their pets down, this rarely if ever happens! It may be that despite a normal activity level after spaying and neutering, removal of the sex hormones in some way encourages fat deposition, but this is speculative at this point.

Certainly obese dogs can have diseases such as hypothyroidism or diabetes, but metabolic diseases are uncommon causes of obesity in dogs, making up approximately 5 percent or less of the pets with weight problems. In hypothyroidism, dogs cannot make enough thyroid hormone. Thyroid hormone is an important hormone that regulates proper metabolism. With too little thyroid hormone, the pet's metabolism is reduced and obesity can result.

Many diabetic dogs and cats are obese. Some with chronic disease show weight loss but rarely emaciation. In diabetes, the dog cannot make enough insulin to regulate the blood sugar glucose. As a result, the blood glucose level rises. In people, we know that obesity is related to diabetes as insulin reserves can become exhausted. This link has not been firmly investigated or established in dogs and cats to my knowledge, although there may be some relationship.

Every obese dog should be screened for problems such as hypothyroidism or diabetes. In my own practice, it is rare that an overweight pet has either of these conditions or any medical problems that are directly related to the weight problem. Occasionally I will even give a trial dose of thyroid hormone to see whether that will help reduce the weight even if the blood level of the thyroid hormone is normal. I do this because, despite normal blood levels of thyroid hormone, some problem or defect can occur at the cellular level. Unfortunately, supplementing with thyroid hormone rarely contributes to the control of obesity.

While we are on the topic of medical problems causing obesity, it is important to differentiate "obesity," which results from fat deposition inside the body as well as under the skin, from "enlargement." Pets can experience abdominal enlargement, for example, from a variety of problems including the adrenal gland disease called Cushing's disease, organ failure (where fluid builds up in the abdominal cavity resulting in a "big belly"), and abdominal tumors. Any time a pet seems larger than normal is a cause for concern that is unlikely related to obesity but very probably related to a serious medical disorder.

> Wild animals do not become fat. They constantly exercise, often go without food for days, and eat a well-balanced diet of natural foods the way nature intended.

But when all is said and done, the main cause of obesity in pets (and pet owners) is overfeeding during puppyhood, adulthood, or both. Obesity is a disease of domestication and greed. Wild animals do not become fat. They constantly exercise, often go without food for days, and eat a well-balanced diet of natural foods the way nature intended. Our sedentary pets that are fed anything they want whenever they want have no choice but to become obese (just like many of their owners). The habit of feeding our puppies and adult dogs whenever they want to eat (or whenever they beg or whenever we use food in training programs) must stop if we are to control their weight.

Can we prevent obesity? Keep in mind that most obese pets are made that way, not born that way. Many years ago I remember reading an article about "Killing Your Pet with Kindness." The eye-opening article discussed how so many owners give their dogs treats and snacks and feed them whenever the dog begs for food. In essence, these owners were setting their pets up for all the medical problems that can occur with obesity. While they thought they were being kind and loving owners, they were actually killing their pets with kindness.

Obesity in pets and people comes in two varieties: increased number of fat cells and increased size of fat cells. Increased food intake in adult pets causes more fat to accumulate in existing fat cells. The number of fat cells do not increase in number but in size.

During puppyhood, which lasts from birth until approximately 12 months in smaller breeds of dogs and up to 24 months in large and giant breeds, overfeeding increases the number of fat cells. Weight reduction is more difficult in pets and people with greater numbers of fat cells. To prevent this type of obesity, young growing animals should not be overfed. I prefer to have owners slightly underfeed these pets. While these pet owners are often scorned by apparently well-meaning friends and family members for "starving" their puppies, they actually are practicing preventive medicine. Slightly underweight, slower-growing puppies will not develop obesity as a result of increased fat cell numbers, which is the more difficult type of obesity to treat. They will also experience fewer skeletal disorders (such as hip dysplasia, shoulder dysplasia, elbow dysplasia, and osteochondrosis) so commonly seen in fast-growing, large breeds of dogs.

Since most commercial pet food recommendations result in young animals being overfed, owners should feed their puppies anywhere from 5 percent (for smaller breeds) up to 15 percent (for larger breeds) less food than recommended if they choose to feed a premium, natural processed food.

Because leaner, more muscular animals have higher metabolic rates than their counterparts with less body musculature, maintaining an exercise program will also contribute to a lean body. The higher metabolic rate burns more calories. If you have an obese pet, you must take steps to control her weight before problems develop. The treatment of obesity requires a controlled low-calorie, lowfat diet with a sensible exercise program. Nutritional supplements might help reduce weight in selected patients.

Problems Caused by Obesity

Numerous problems are associated with obesity in pets— and people. These include orthopedic problems such as arthritis, ruptured ligaments, intervertebral disk disease, breathing difficulty, reduced ability to exercise, heat intolerance, increased chance for complications due to drug therapy (because it is more difficult to accurately dose medications in obese pets), cardiac problems, hypertension, and cancer. When you keep in mind that the excess body fat occurs in the body cavities of the chest and abdomen (often being deposited there first), as well as under the skin (what we see as "fat"), all the medical problems associated with obesity are not surprising. As the owner of a dog that limps, you must understand that obesity is a major contributing factor in causing discomfort in pets with arthritis.

Obesity is often present in arthritic pets. An important part of the treatment for these pets is to get them to lose weight. Extra weight carried by diseased joints adds to the wear and tear on the joints and the pain and discomfort your pet will experience (not to mention other health problems caused by obesity, such as heart and lung disease). Weight loss is a desired goal in the treatment of the arthritic pet.

PROPER WEIGHT LOSS

A SENSIBLE WEIGHT-LOSS program encourages slow, controlled loss of excessive body fat. For the truly overweight dog, a medically controlled obesity-reduction diet is needed. Obesity must be controlled in arthritic pets; otherwise whatever therapy approach is chosen will be inadequate and possibly futile. Because obesity has several causes, and because obesity may be associated with various serious medical conditions, an overweight dog should undergo a thorough diagnostic work-up, including blood and urine tests. Pets with underlying medical problems, such as hypothyroidism, will not lose weight unless the medical problems are addressed.

Realize that obesity does not occur overnight, and neither will it go away overnight. While a very small subset of pets truly cannot lose weight, most pets will reach an acceptable weight within 6 to 12 months of starting an obesity diet coupled with an approved exercise program. This rate of weight loss approximates 2 percent per week, which is an acceptable amount that will not cause muscle loss. The actual rate of weight loss recommended by your veterinarian may vary according to your pet's needs.

Prior to starting a weight-reduction diet and exercise regimen, it is important that your pet receive a blood profile to rule out diseases we have discussed (diabetes or hypothyroidism, for example) that may cause or contribute to obesity. Presence of these diseases would require treatment in addition to dietary therapy.

Also, since various diseases including diabetes and hypothyroidism can cause or contribute to obesity, it is imperative to test for these diseases prior to starting a medically controlled weight-loss program.

If your dog needs to lose weight, he should be on a weight-reduction diet recommended by your veterinarian. Store-bought "lite" foods are not designed for weight loss, but rather weight maintenance once weight loss has been achieved; therefore, they are not usually recommended for pets requiring weight loss. Additionally, since most of these diets do not contain natural healthy ingredients, it is unlikely they would be recommended as part of a weight-loss program unless other diets could not be used.

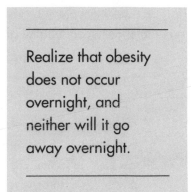

Realize that obesity does not occur overnight, and neither will it go away overnight.

Several commercial weight-loss or obesity reduction diets are available for dogs. However, since many commercial diets contain artificial ingredients and by-products, and since many owners prefer to feed a more natural diet, a recipe that you can use for this purpose is included in the section below.

Simply feeding your pet less food will not result in body fat loss and may result in excessive muscle wasting, weakness, excessive hunger, and other problems.

Any food (including carbohydrate and proteins) can be converted to and stored as fat if not needed by the body for another metabolic process. Feeding fat is more likely to

WEIGHT-CONTROL RECIPE
FOR ADULT DOGS

This recipe, adapted from one offered by D. R. Strombeck in *Home-Prepared Dog and Cat Diets* (Iowa State University Press, Ames, Iowa, 1999) can be used to provide weight loss in a healthy obese dog that should weigh 45 to 50 pounds. This diet should be used only under your veterinarian's supervision.

This daily diet provides approximately 642 kilocalories, 49.4 grams of protein and 5 grams of fat.

½ pound cooked chicken, lowfat beef, venison, or
    rabbit, or 4 egg whites (cooked) or ½ cup 1% fat
    cottage cheese
2 cups cooked long-grain rice or 3 cups cooked
    potatoes (with or without skins)
¼ teaspoon salt or salt substitute
1 multivitamin and mineral tablet
4 bonemeal tablets
2 omega-3 fatty acid capsules

If desired, you can add fresh vegetables (raw or lightly steamed) to the recipe. One-half cup of vegetables add about 30 kilocalories to the diet, with no added fat.

Do not use a vitamin-mineral supplement without veterinary supervision in order to make sure you are not providing too few or too many (toxic) levels of vitamins and minerals. Your veterinarian may prescribe increased levels of certain vitamins, including antioxidants and vitamins C and D, that may be beneficial for the arthritic pet. Good vitamin-mineral supplements for dogs include Catalyn (made by Standard Process) and Canine Plus (made by VetriScience). Four calcium lactate or calcifood wafers (standard process) can substitute for bone meal.

The level of fatty acid in this recipe is a recommended maintenance dose. Your doctor can prescribe a higher therapeutic dose for your arthritic pet.

The inclusion of omega-3 fatty acids adds few calories to the diet, approximately 10 kilocalories depending upon the brand. Because fatty acids can be helpful for arthritic pets, and because they also increase the pet's metabolic rate (which burns calories), they are needed in the diets of obese arthritic pets.

I recommend feeding this recipe or any weight-reduction diet in at least two and preferably four to six meals throughout the day. Frequent small meals allow the pet to feel full all of the time. Feeling full reduces appetite and the need to beg. Begging dogs have been have been unintentionally rewarded by their owners for this behavior. Frequent feeding results in more burning of calories and weight loss.

contribute to fat deposition in fat cells than feeding protein or carbohydrates. Therefore, lower fat diets are preferred for weight loss in pets.

Foods that increase metabolism—such as vegetables, which are high in fiber—are included in weight-loss diets. Fiber contained in vegetables decreases fat and glucose absorption; in turn, the fluctuating glucose levels cause greater insulin release. Since insulin is needed for fat storage, decreased or stable levels (which fiber achieves) are preferred. Fiber also binds to fat in the intestinal tract and increases movement of the food in the intestines, which benefits the obese pet.

Weight-Control Supplements

What about supplements? Are there any supplements to help "burn fat"? Unfortunately there are no magic pills that will ensure weight loss in pets. Still, you can consider some of the supplements listed below that may contribute to weight loss when used as part of a comprehensive plan.

Chromium. Chromium is a trace mineral that can increase the body's sensitivity to insulin. Since decrease sensitivity to insulin can contribute to weight gain (as often happens in diabetic patients), supplying additional chromium (usually at a dose of 200 to 400 mcg/day) is recommended for weight control in people. Research is needed to determine whether chromium would benefit overweight pets.

Carnitine. In people, carnitine is recommended at 500 mg per day to reduce fat deposits. Research is needed to determine this recommendation would be of benefit to overweight dogs.

Boron. This trace mineral may speed up the burning of calories in people.

Herbs. Herbs such as cayenne, mustard, and ginger increase metabolism in people and may also do the same in pets. Your doctor can prescribe a safe dose of these herbs if he feels they might help your pet.

Hydroxycitric Acid. Hydroxycitric acid, also called HCA, is a product extracted from the rind of the tamarind citrus fruit of the *Garcinia cambogia* tree. It suppresses hunger in people and helps prevent the body from turning carbohydrates into fat by inhibiting the ATP-citrate lysase enzyme (the recommended dosage is 500 mg 3 times daily). While it is available for use in people, I have not seen any reported doses or studies showing its use in pets (early studies showed effectiveness in chickens and rats). Your veterinarian might be able to extrapolate a dose for use in your overweight dog if he or she feels the product might be of benefit. Alternatively, the supplement Nutriweight can be used as part of an obesity management program (see page 194).

Chitosan. Chitosan is a dietary supplement made from the outer skeletons of shellfish. The product is purported to bind to fat in the intestines, which prevents the absorption of fat. Studies are inconclusive regarding how well the product works in people or pets. One veterinary company is currently developing a product containing chitosan. Time will tell whether it will be of value in any diet programs for pets.

Coenzyme Q10. Coenzyme Q10 is used to transport and break down fat into energy. In people, coenzyme Q10 levels were found to be low in approximately 50 percent of obese individuals. Supplementing with coenzyme Q10 resulted in accelerated weight loss in overweight people. While coenzyme Q10 is often used in pets with heart disease, periodontal disease, and gastrointestinal disease, I have not seen any reports showing its use as part of a weight-control program. It may, however, benefit overweight pets. At the recommended dosage, no side effects have been seen. Consult with your doctor about using coenzyme Q10 to help in a weight-reduction program for your pet.

Currently, one supplement is formulated for use as part of a weight-management program for pets. NutriWeightR, made by RxVitamins for Pets, contains HCA as the main "fat-burning" nutrient. The manufacturer markets the product as a formula that contains "phytonutrients, fat-burning nutrients, minerals, and nutritional cofactors that assist in the maintenance of optimal weight." I have not seen any controlled studies confirming its effectiveness, although anecdotal reports indicate it may help pets lose weight. The product should be safe and could be used under veterinary supervision in a weight-loss program.

Certain processed foods contain "therapeutic" amounts of omega fatty acids and other nutrients. Even if pets don't respond to these supplements, using one of these special diets may be beneficial. Your veterinarian can prescribe one of these diets if it is necessary.

Supplements to Avoid

Supplements and medications that are not recommended for weight loss in dogs include diuretics and appetite suppressants such as phenylpropanolamine and caffeine. Diuretics, often used for weight loss in people, cause increased urination (followed by increased water consumption) and only temporarily result in weight loss due to water loss. You probably do not cherish the thought of your dog urinating all the time. Since this practice is unappealing and can upset your pet's balance of electrolytes, which can be dangerous, using diuretics for obese pets is not recommended.

Phenylpropanolamine is a stimulant, appetite suppressant, and decongestant. While it will increase blood pressure and jitteriness, it is not effective for long-term weight loss in people, nor is it recommended for this purpose with pets.

Caffeine is a mild stimulant that may exhibit a fat-burning effect. However, since caffeine may contribute to jitteriness and hyperactivity, its use is not recommended for weight control in pets.

Why Weight-Control Programs Fail

Despite the owner's best efforts, some diet programs just don't seem to work. I believe there are three reason for this: disease, doctor involvement, and owner patience.

While an underlying disorder such as Cushing's disease (a thyroid disease) is only present in at most 5 percent of obese dogs, all obese patients should be screened for this and other diseases prior to starting a comprehensive weight-reduction program. Failure to do so could result in no weight loss and potential serious illness or death in the patient who has such a condition.

Many owners decide to implement a weight-reduction program on their own without proper veterinary supervision. Lack of doctor involvement may doom the weight-control approach for several reasons. First, in those rare cases with underlying medical disorders causing or contributing to the obesity, the true problem will not be diagnosed and the diet will not work.

Second, most owner-implemented diet programs simply consist of the owner feeding a "lite" diet or just "feeding less." As we have discussed, lite diets are basically worthless for weight-loss programs. Feeding less rarely results in weight loss because pets that eat less are hungrier, beg more, and ultimately are fed more as the owners become impatient from the constant begging for food. When pets (and people) eat less, their metabolism slows down. Pets that are fed less will adapt to this lower metabolism and maintain weight.

> Weight control must be an important consideration as part of an arthritis prevention approach for dogs.

What about starving the pet? Most owners do not want to see their pets starve, and we certainly must question whether or not this procedure is humane. Starvation will reduce fat but also burn muscle. People who starve can develop medical complications due to deranged glucose and fat metabolism. While this may not be as much of a problem in dogs (unlike in cats, in which serious fatty liver disease can develop within a matter of days), starvation is not recommended, as significant metabolic problems could arise in dogs that are starved.

Owner patience also comes into play concerning the time it takes the dog to lose the extra pounds. Obesity does not happen overnight, and neither does weight loss. Owners must be patient, especially with larger dogs that might require many months of eating a proper diet in order to slowly lose weight.

Regardless of how helpful supplements may be in weight loss, they are no substitute for a lifestyle change. Remember, obesity adds to the stress on damaged joints for our arthritic pets. Therefore, weight control must be an important consideration as part of an arthritis prevention approach for dogs.

HIP DYSPLASIA

HIP DYSPLASIA HAS been discussed as a cause of lameness and trigger for arthritis. Here I will briefly review what it is, how it is diagnosed, and how early surgery to correct hip dysplasia can prevent future arthritis. With hip dysplasia, the hips are unstable as a result of genetic factors, environmental factors, or both. Some young puppies show signs of hip dysplasia before 12 months of age. These dogs have difficulty rising and often walk with a swayed gait in the rear legs. Pain may be present as the owners manipulate the legs. Dogs can be screened for this condition very early in life. Dogs that text positive for dysplasia should not be bred. While many owners are familiar with the screening for breeding dogs at 2 years of age, many owners are surprised that puppies can be screened even earlier in life.

To check for hip dysplasia, puppies are radiographed while under anesthesia. This can be done while the puppy is under anesthesia for another reason. In my practice I routinely screen puppies brought in for spaying and neutering. Surprisingly, 60 to 70 percent of puppies I've screened for hip dysplasia actually have the condition. Remember that these are "normal" puppies with no clinical history. They are walking and playing normally. I also attempt to physically "pop" the hips out of joint. I know this sounds unkind, but after we pop the hips out of joint, they go right back in at the end of the evaluation and the pet never feels any aftereffects. The reason for early screening is that if the pet has signs of hip dysplasia, surgery to repair or replace the joint is available. If the owner chooses to have the problem corrected early, it would be very rare for arthritis of the hips to develop later in life. This then, is one type of arthritic condition that can be prevented early in life, either through surgery or careful screening of parents prior to breeding.

ANTIOXIDANTS

CAN ANTIOXIDANTS SUCH as vitamin C actually prevent arthritis and skeletal problems in pets? This is a common question from pet owners who want to prevent the common problem of hip dysplasia and secondary osteoarthritis in their puppies. What does the research show?

You may recall reading in chapter 5 about Dr. Wendell Belfield's research on eight litters of German shepherd puppies born to dysplastic or dysplastic-producing parents. From his studies, Dr. Belfield concluded that vitamin C can be used to prevent and treat pets with hip dysplasia and other joint conditions including osteochondrosis and osteoarthritis. Dr. Daniel Richardson, however, concluded that no evidence supports Dr. Belfield's conclusion. Whether vitamin C is or isn't effective in preventing arthritis in pets requires further scientific research.

Since vitamin C is a safe vitamin, however, you may wish to incorporate it into a regimen to help dogs with arthritis. Ask your veterinarian to recommend the proper dosage if he feels vitamin C may benefit your dog.

CHAPTER SUMMARY

- It is possible to prevent some forms of arthritis.

- Obesity is a contributing cause of arthritis in pets, and pet owners.

- Prevent obesity in your dog by establishing healthy eating habits from puppyhood.

- If your dog is obese, work with your veterinarian to establish a proper weight-control program.

- Have your dog tested for hip dysplasia during puppyhood to prevent the onset of arthritis.

- Antioxidants may prevent and treat joint diseases in dogs.

·10·

Tying It
All Together

As WE COME to the end of this book, I hope you have a better understanding of canine arthritis. Remember that this condition takes months to years to evolve, and is a painful and inflammatory condition. Remember, too, that causes other than arthritis, such as neurological disorders and cancers, result in lameness of pets; therefore, a proper diagnosis is essential before choosing any therapy for your lame pet.

While conventional medications such as corticosteroids and non-steroidal anti-inflammatory medications do have their place in the treatment of some arthritic dogs, these drugs result in too many potential side effects to use them as the sole, long-term therapy for any but the very few dogs that do not improve with any other treatment.

Complementary therapies such as nutritional supplements, acupuncture, and homeopathy all have their place in the treatment of the pet with arthritis. At times they can serve as the sole therapy, although we'll often combine them with lower doses of conventional medications to help the pet.

To tie all these ideas together, here is my holistic approach to the arthritic dog:

• *Provide your dog a healthy life.* Feed your pet a wholesome and natural nutritious diet from puppyhood and practice an exercise program suited for the size, age, and energy level of your dog.

• *Establish a relationship with a holistic veterinarian for the regular care of your pet.* All approaches are more successful when the dog is comfortable with medical procedures and the veterinarian is acquainted with the dog.

• *Obtain a correct diagnosis for your lame dog.* Because osteoarthritis is a degenerative process, the earlier a correct diagnosis is made and the proper treatment is started, the sooner you can attempt to make your pet feel better and slow the destruction of the joint.

• *Have your dog tested for hip dysplasia in puppyhood.* This is often best done while the dog is under anesthesia for neutering.

• *Have proper radiographs taken.* Once you find the location and cause of the lameness or pain, and are comfortable that you are not dealing with other causes of lameness such as immune causes of joint destruction, infectious arthritis, neurological diseases, or cancer, get professional diagnostic testing. This usually involves radiographs of the affected bones and joints, often taken under heavy sedation or anesthesia because of the uncomfortable, possibly painful positions the dog must assume for his doctor to fully evaluate the joints.

• *Get additional tests performed.* Ancillary diagnostic testing, such as blood and urine testing, may be needed to make sure that internal diseases are not causing the clinical signs. Also, since many of these pets are older animals, diagnosing and treating coexisting conditions is important. And if drug therapy such as non-steroidal medications must be given, make sure that underlying problems that could worsen with conventional medicines (such as kidney or liver disease) are not present.

• *Discuss your option with a holistic-minded veterinarian.* For pets with osteoarthritis, I discuss the numerous treatment options with the owner. Dogs that are in severe pain are often treated with traditional medical therapy, such as short-term therapy with low doses of corticosteroids or non-steroidal medications to give quick relief. Most if not all pets are placed on oral nutritional supplements. Pets with severely debilitating osteoarthritis are often started on weekly injections of chondroprotective agents to achieve a faster result while waiting for the oral supplements to "kick in."

• *Use nutritional supplements.* For long-term therapy, I have a lot of success with nutritional therapies using products containing glucosamine and chondroitin plus omega-3 fatty acids and raw food and glandular supplements. Most of my patients are maintained on this regimen without side effects. Occasionally I add homeopathy, acupuncture, or conventional medications if the pet is having a "bad day."

• *Use acupuncture or homeopathy in addition to nutritional and other supplements.* If nutritional therapies don't give your dog the desired results, keep the pet on the products to help heal the joint but use acupuncture or homeopathy or both to aid in decreasing inflammation and pain.

• *Use acupuncture or homeopathy in place of conventional therapies for long-term care.* In place of long-term therapy with conventional drugs, consider acupuncture or homeopathy on an "as needed" basis to give the pet relief from pain.

• *Continue your dog's healthy lifestyle.* Feed your dog a proper diet to control weight and maintain vigor. Practice exercise options that do not contribute to her pain. Provide your dog the tenderness she deserves with physical therapies such as massage, heat, and joint manipulation that ease her pain.

Every doctor develops his or her favorite approach to dealing with various disorders such as arthritis. To treat the pet holistically, trying to do what's best for the pet's overall health and well-being is important. The pet must be treated humanely, and you should be involved in all treatment decisions for your dog.

There is no hard and fast rule to use when deciding what treatment is best for a particular dog. I explain options to the owners, including side effects and costs of the treatments. We then form a team with the goal of doing what's best for the pet. When owners are involved in treatment decisions, they are more likely to take an interest in the therapy. Additionally, they feel important to the pet's outcome and are vital treatment team members. This approach is far different from that of the doctor who sees himself as "God" and uses "shotgun" therapy with no owner involvement. Pet owners are loving, dedicated, kind-hearted people. It is essential that they be involved in the decision-making process, as they are ultimately responsible for their pets.

For more information about holistic pet care for pets, or to find a holistic veterinarian in your area, contact the American Holistic Veterinary Medical Association at 410-569-0795 and visit the Pet Care Naturally Web site at www.petcarenaturally.com.

BIBLIOGRAPHY

Ackerman, L. "Reviewing the Biochemical Properties of Fatty Acids." *Veterinary Medicine* (Dec. 1995): 1138-1148.

Ackerman, L. "Dermatologic Uses of Fatty Acids in Dogs and Cats." *Veterinary Medicine* (Dec. 1995): 1149-1155.

Ackerman, L. "Nondermatologic Indications for Fatty Acid Supplementation in Dogs and Cats." *Veterinary Medicine* (Dec. 1995): 1156-1159.

Altman, S. "Small Animal Acupuncture: Scientific Basis and Clinical Applications." In *Complementary and Alternative Veterinary Medicine: Principles and Practice*, edited by A. Schoen and S. Wynn. Mosby: St. Louis, (1998): 147-168.

Anderson, M. A., M. R. Slater, and T. A. Hammad. "Results of a Survey of Small Animal Practitioners on the Perceived Clinical Efficacy and Safety of an Oral Nutraceutical." *Preventative Veterinary Medicine* 38, (1999): 65-73.

Balch, J. and P. Balch. *Prescription for Nutritional Healing*. Avery Publishing, 1997.

Bardet, J. F. "Lameness." In the *Textbook of Veterinary Internal Medicine*. 4th ed. W. B. Saunders: Philadelphia, (1995): 136-143.

Belfield, W. "Worthomolecular Medicine: A Practitioner's Perspective." In *Complementary and Alternative Veterinary Medicine: Principles and Practice*, edited by A. Schoen and S. Wynn. Mosby: St. Louis, (1998): 113-132.

Bennett, D. and C. May. "Joint Diseases of Dogs and Cats." In *Textbook of Veterinary Internal Medicine*. 4th ed. W. B. Saunders: Philadelphia, (1995): 2032–2077.

Bennett, D. "Treatment of the Immune-Mediated Inflammatory Arthropathies of the Dog and Cat." *Current Veterinary Therapy XI*. W. B. Saunders: Philadelphia, (1995): 1188–1195.

Beren, J. J., S. L. Hill, and N. R. Rose. "Therapeutic Effects of CosaminR on Autoimmune Type II Collagen Induced Arthritis in Rats." North American Veterinary Conference, 1997.

Bratman, S. and D. Kroll. *Natural Health Bible*. Prima Publishing, 1999.

Chen, J. *Clinical Manual of Oriental Medicine*. Lotus Herbs, 1999.

D'Ambrosia, E., B. Casa, G. Bompani, et al. "Glucosamine Suplate: A Controlled Clinical Evaluation in Arthroisis." *Pharmatherapeutica* 2 (1981): 504.

Day, C. *The Homeopathic Treatment of Small Animals*. C. W. Daniel: Essex, 1990.

Day, C. and J. G. G. Saxton. "Veterinarian Homeopathy: Principles and Practice." In *Complementary and Alternative Veterinary Medicine: Principles and Practice*, edited by A. Schoen and S. Wynn. Mosby: St. Louis, (1998): 485–514.

DeCava, J. "Glandular Supplements." In *Nutrition News and Views*, May/June 1997. PO Box 877, West Barnstable, MA 02668-0877.

De Guzman, E. "Western Herbal Medicine: Clinical Applications." In *Complementary and Alternative Veterinary Medicine: Principles and Practice*, edited by A. Schoen and S. Wynn. Mosby: St. Louis, (1998): 337–378.

Frost, M. *Going Back to the Basics of Human Health*. International Foundation for Nutrition and Health, 1997.

Gibson, R. G. "Homeopathic Therapy in Rheumatoid Arthritis: Evaluation by Double-Blind Clinical Therapeutic Trial." *British Journal of Clinical Pharmacology* (May 1980): 453–459.

Grazi, S. and M. Costa. *SAMe (S-adenosylmethionine)*. Prima Publishing, 1999.

Hobbs, R. and G. Bucco. *Everything You Need to Know About Arthritis*. Prima Publishing, 1999.

Hudson, Donald and Doreen Hudson. "Magnetic Field Therapy." In *Complementary and Alternative Veterinary Medicine: Principles and Practice*, edited by A. Schoen and S. Wynn. Mosby: St. Louis, (1998): 275-296.

Hulse, D. S., D. Hart, M. Slatter, and B. S. Beale. "The Effect of Cosequin in Cranial Cruciate Deficient and Reconstructed Stifle Joints in Dogs." Veterinary Orthopedic Society 25th Annual Conference, February 1998: 64.

Johnson, K. and A. D. J Watson. "Skeletal Diseases." In the *Textbook of Veterinary Internal Medicine*. 4th ed. W. B. Saunders: Philadelphia, 1995.

Johnson, K. "Treatment of Osteomyelitis, Discospondylitis, and Septic Arthritis." In *Bonagura J. Kirk's Current Veterinary Therapy XII*. W. B. Saunders: Philadelphia, (1995): 1200-1204.

Kandel, J. and D. Sudderth. *The Arthritis Solution*. Prima Publishing, 1997.

Kendall, R. "Therapeutic Nutrition for the Cat, Dog, and Horse." In *Complementary and Alternative Veterinary Medicine: Principles and Practice,* edited by A. Schoen and S. Wynn. Mosby: St. Louis, (1998): 53-72.

Lane, I. W. and E. Contreras, Jr. "High rate of Bioactivity (Reduction in Gross Tumor Size) Observed in Advanced Cancer Patients Treated With Shark Cartilage Material." *Journal of Naturopathic Medicine* 1992, (3) 1:86-88.

Lane, I. W. and L. Comac. *Sharks Don't Get Cancer*. Avery Publishing, 1993.

Lane, I. W. "Shark Cartilage: Its Potential Medical Applications." *Journal of Advancement in Medicine*, vol 4, no 4 (1991): 263-271.

Lees, P. "Inflammation and the Pharmacology of Anti-inflammatory Drugs." In *New Advances in Control of Pain and Inflammation.* Proceedings of the ACVIM, (1997): 7–20.

Lewis, L., M. Morris, Jr., and M. Hand. *Small Animal Clinical Nutrition.* 4th ed. Mark Morris Association: Topeka, 2000.

Lopes, A. "Double-blind Clinical Evaluation of the Relative Efficacy of Ibuprofen and Glucosamine Suplate in the Management of Osteoarthrosis of the knee in outpatients." *Current Medical Res. and Opinion* 8 (1982): 145.

Macleod, G. *Dogs: Homeopathic Remedies.* C.W. Daniel: Essex, 1992.

Magne, M. "Swollen Joints and Lameness." In the *Textbook of Veterinary Internal Medicine.* 5th ed. W.B. Saunders: Philadelphia, (1999): 77–79.

Manley, P. "The Treatment of Degenerative Joint Disease." In *Bonagura J. Kirk's Current Veterinary Therapy XII.* W. B. Saunders: Philadelphia, (1995): 1196–1199.

Matz, M. "Gastrointestinal Ulcer Therapy." *Current Veterinary Therapy XII.* W. B. Saunders: Philadelphia, (1995): 706–710.

McDonald, R., and V. Langston. "Use of Corticosteroids and Nonsteroidal anti-inflammatory Agents." In the *Textbook of Veterinary Internal Medicine.* 4th ed. W. B. Saunders: Philadelphia, (1995): 284–293.

McNamara, P., S. Barr, and H. Erb. "Hematologic, Hemostatic, and Biochemical Effects in Dogs Receiving an Oral Chondroprotective Agent for Thirty Days." *AJVR,* vol 57, no 9. (Sept. 1996): 1390–1394.

Moore, K. "LLT for the Treatment of Chronic Pain." *Frontiers in Electro-Optics.* Conference Proceedings, 1990: 283–290.

Morrison, R. "Magnetic Healing." *Dog and Kennel.* (October 1999): 36–38.

Murray, M. and J. Pizzorno. *Encyclopedia of Natural Medicine.* 2nd ed. Prima Publishing, 1998.

Murray, M. *The Healing Power of Herbs*. Prima Publishing, (1995): 378-379.

Murray, R. *Natural vs. Synthetic, Life vs. Death, Truth vs. the Lie*. Standard Process, 1995.

Papich, M., E. Hardie. "Management of Chronic Pain." In *New Advances in Control of Pain and Inflammation*. Proceedings of the ACVIM, 1997: 61-70.

Pedersen, N., H. Morgan, and P. Vasseur. "Joint Diseases of Dogs and Cats." In the *Textbook of Veterinary Internal Medicine*. 5th ed. W. B. Saunders: Philadelphia, (1999): 1862-1886.

Phillipi, A., C. Leffler, and S. Leffler. "Glucosamine Chondroitin, and Manganese Ascorbate for Degenerative Joint Disease of the Knee or Low Back: A Randomized Double-blind Placebo-controlled Study." *Military Medicine*, vol 164, (Feb 1999): 85-91.

Pitcairn, R. and S. Pitcairn. *Dr. Pitcairn's Complete Guide to Natural Health for Dogs and Cats*. Rodale, (1995): 235-236.

Plumb, D. *Veterinary Drug Handbook*. 3rd ed. Iowa State University Press: Ames, (1999): 102-103; 260-261; 306-308; and 528-535.

Richardson, D. "Developmental Orthopedics: Nutritional Influences in the Dog." In the *Textbook of Veterinary Internal Medicine*. 4th ed. W. B. Saunders: Philadelphia, (1995): 252-257.

Rosenfeld, I. *Dr. Rosenfeld's Guide to Alternative Medicine*. Random House, (1996): 208-216.

Schoen, A. M. "Acupuncture for Musculoskeletal Disorders." In *Veterinary Acupuncture*. Mosby: Chicago, 1994.

Schwartz, C. "Chinese Herbal Medicine in Small Animal Practice." In *Complementary and Alternative Veterinary Medicine: Principles and Practice*. Mosby: St. Louis, (1998): 437-450.

Schrader, S. "The Use of Laboratory in the Diagnosis of Joint Disorders of Dogs and Cats." *Current Veterinary Therapy XII*. W. B. Saunders: Philadelphia, (1995): 1166-1171.

Schrader, S. "Differential Diagnosis of Non-traumatic Causes of Lameness in Young Growing Dogs." In *Current Veterinary Therapy XII.* W. B. Saunders: Philadelphia, (1995): 1171–1180.

Smith, G., and P. McKelvie. "Current Concepts in the Diagnosis of Canine Hip Dysplasia." *Current Veterinary Therapy XII.* W. B. Saunders: Philadelphia, (1995): 1180–1188.

Strazza, M. "Magnetic Field Exposure as an Adjunct Therapeutic Modality in the Dog, Cat, and Horse." *Journal of the American Holistic Veterinary Medical Association,* May/July 1996, vol 15, no 2: 27–31.

Strombeck, D. *Home-Prepared Dog and Cat Diets.* Iowa State University Press, (1999): 217–236.

Thompson, J. "Immunologic Diseases." *Textbook of Veterinary Internal Medicine.* 4th ed. W. B. Saunders: Philadelphia, (1995): 2002–2029.

Tilford, G. and M. Wulff-Tilford. *All You Ever Wanted to Know About Herbs for Pets.* BowTie Press: Irvine, (1999): 66–68; 170–173; 264–269.

Ullman, D. "Homeopathic Medicine: Principles and Research." *Complementary and Alternative Veterinary Medicine: Principles and Practice,* edited by Schoen and Wynn. Mosby: St. Louis, (1998): 469–484.

Whitaker, J. *Dr. Whitaker's Guide to Natural Healing.* Prima Publishing, 1996.

Wilson, J. "Shark Cartilage: A Review of Background Literature and Research." *Townsend Letter for Doctors,* Aug/Sept 1994.

Wolfsheimer, K. "Obesity." *Textbook of Veterinary Internal Medicine.* 5th ed. W. B. Saunders: Philadelphia, (1999): 70–71.

INDEX

Abdominal enlargement, 185
ACE inhibitors, 77
Acetaminophen, 68
  toxicity of, 81–82
Acetylator (Vetri-Science), 120
Actaea rac, 144
Acupressure, 177
Acupuncture, xii, 87, 134–137, 201
  for cauda equina syndrome, 19
  for disk disease, 17, 18
  for panosteitis, 36
  reaction of animals to, 136
  for rheumatoid arthritis, 23
  side effects, 135–136
  for soft tissue injuries, 16
  use of, 203–204
  for Wobbler's Syndrome, 19
Acupuncture and Holistic Animal
    Health Care Center, vii
Additives in processed foods, 157–160
Adequan, 113
Adrenocorticotrophic hormone
    (ACT), 62
Adult Attention Deficit Disorder, 99
Advil, 69
Aging dogs. See Geriatric dogs
Aleve, 69
Alfalfa, 92–93, 128
  in health formulas, 97–98
Algae, 92–93
Allergies
  chemicals in processed foods
    and, 160
  fatty acids and, 96

Alpha-linoleic acid (ALA), 95
Alternative therapies, xiii–xiv
American Association of Feed Con-
    trol Officials (AAFCO), 155
American Holistic Veterinary Med-
    ical Association, 43, 204
Amylase, 90, 92
Anaprox, 69
Anemia
  lupus causing, 21
  non-steroidal anti-inflammatories
    (NSAIDS) and, 77
Animal Protection Institute
  on preservatives in processed
    foods, 158
  Web site, 154
Ankles, 6
  osteochondrosis in, 34
Ansaid, 69
Anti-caking chemicals, 160–161
Antioxidants, 98–104, 198
  colon growths and, 102
  in processed foods, 158, 160
Aquapuncture, 134
Arachidonic acid, 9, 60, 70–71
  inflammation and, 94
Ark Naturals, 121
Arthri-Nu (VPL), 120
The Arthritis Solution, 172–173
Arthroscopy, 54
Arthrose (King Pharmacy), 120
Arthrotec, 69
Arthrotomy, 54
Articular cartilage, 6, 8

Artificial coloring in processed foods, 158
Aspirin. *See* Non-steroidal anti-inflammatories (NSAIDS)
Astragalus, 131
Ataxia, 18
Atlantoaxial dislocation, 28, 29
ATP molecule, 119
Autoimmune diseases, 20, 21–26
AziumR, 67

Banamine, 69
BARF diet, 163–167
Barley grass, 92–93, 169
  in health formulas, 97–98
Basset hounds, 28
Beche de mer, 107
Belfield, Wendell, 100–101, 198
Bennett, David, 81
Bernese mountain dogs, 26
Betamethasone, 67
Bilberry, 98
Billinghurst, Ian, 163
Billinghurst diet, 163–167
Bioflavonoids, 99
Biotherapies, 120
Biotin, 92
Black currant oil, 93
Blood tests, 51–53, 202–203
  for hepatosoonosis, 31–32
  for Lyme disease, 30–31
Body composition score, 182–183
Bonemeal, 168
Bones
  cancer of, 26–27
  dogs eating, 166
  infections of, 2–3
  scans of, 51
  tumors of, 2
Borage oil, 93
Boron, 192
Boswellia, 128
Bovine cartilage, 105–106
  hyaluronic acid (HA) from, 113

Boxers, 176
Breathing difficulty, 187
Brewer's yeast, 169
Bromelain, 115, 133
Bruises, 16
Bryonia, 144
Bucco, G., 69, 95, 111
Bull mastiffs, 28
Butazolidin, 69
Butylated hydroxtoluene (BHT), 158, 159
Butylated hydroxyansole (BHA), 158, 159

Caffeine, 194, 195
Calcified disks, 18
Calcarea carbonica, 144
Calcifood (Standard Process), 103, 191
Calcium
  in barley grass, 92
  in homemade diets, 168
  osteochondrosis and, 33
Calcium Lactate (Standard Process), 103
Calcium lactate wafers, 103, 191
Cancer, 20, 26–27
  chemicals in processed foods and, 160
  colon cancer, 102
  obesity and, 187
  processed foods, cancer-causing agents in, 159
  slaughterhouse wastes, feeding, 155–156
Cani-Flex (Vet-A-Mix), 120
Canine Plus (Vetri-Science), 191
Capsaicin/cayenne, 128, 133
  for weight-control, 193
Carbohydrates in processed foods, 156–157
Carbonate, 168
Carcinogens in processed foods, 159
Cardiac problems, 187

Carnitine, 192
Carprofen, 58-59
    cartilage damage and, 77-79
    gastrointestinal bleeding from,
        71
    incidence of side effects, 80
    liver disease and, 76-77
    side effects, 58-59, 73-76
    toxicity of, 82
Cartiflex (VRx), 120
Cartilage. *See also* Chondroprotec-
    tive supplements
    cells, 8
    corticosteroids and, 65
    non-steroidal anti-inflammatories
        (NSAIDS) and, 77-79
Cartivet (Biotherapies), 120
Cataflam, 69
Catalyn (Standard Process), 103,
    191
Cataplex B/C/G (Standard Process),
    103
Cat Fancy magazine, viii
Cats
    obesity in, 181, 182
    onion toxicity, 157
    starvation in, 196
    thiamine deficiency in, 151
Cauda equina syndrome, 19, 28
Caulophyllum, 144
Cayenne. *See* Capsaicin/cayenne
Celebrex, 69, 72
Celecoxib, 69
Celluase, 92
Cetyl myristoleate, 118-119
Chemicals in processed foods,
    160-161
Chicken in processed foods, 155
Chihuahuas
    atlantoaxial dislocation, 28
    shoulder dislocation, 28, 29
Chinese herbal therapy, 126-127
    formulas in, 130-131
    guidelines for, 126
Chitosan for weight-control, 193

Chlorophyll, 92-93
    in barley grass, 92
Cholesterol, 13
    fatty acids and, 93
Choline, 92
Chondrocytes, 8, 105
Chondroitin, xi, 8, 110-112
    for hip dysplasia, 176
    for osteochondrosis, 34
    for overuse syndrome, 32
    in sea cucumber, 107
    for spondylosis deformans, 36
Chondroprotective supplements,
    87, 104-115
    acupuncture with, 134
    bovine cartilage, 105-106
    bromelain in, 115
    cetyl myristoleate, 118-119
    chondroitin, 110-112
    costs of, 114
    DMG (dimethylglycine), 116-117
    glucosamine, 110-112
    list of, 120-121
    methylsulfonylmethane (MSM),
        117-118
    mullein in, 115
    perna mussels, 106-107
    protocol for use of, 116
    purity of products, 114-115
    SAMe (S-adenosylmethionine),
        119, 122-123
    sea cucumber, 107-108
    shark cartilage, 108-110
    skullcap in, 115
    use of, 112-115
    yucca in, 115-116
Chondrosarcoma, 26
Chromium, 192
Cimetidine, 82
Cinnamon bark, 131
Clematis, 131
Clinoril, 69
Coccidian, 31
Cocker spaniels, 28
Codonopsis, 131

Coenzyme Q10
  as antioxidant, 98
  for weight-control, 193–194
Collagen, 8
  corticosteroids and, 63
Collies, 24–25
Colon cancer, 102
Complementary and Alternative Veterinary Medicine: Principles and Practice (Belfield), 100–101
Complementary therapies, xiii–xiv, 87–124, 201
  for cancer, 27
  for lupus, 22
  patents for, 4
  for polymyositis/polyarthritis, 25
  research on, 3–5
  veterinarians supporting, 39
Congenital disorders, 15, 20, 27–29
Conventional treatments, 59–60
Corticosteroids, xiii, xv, 2, 201
  commonly used corticosteroids, 67
  for disk disease, 17, 18
  duration of effects, 67
  effects of, 61, 63
  long-term side effects, 64
  for lupus, 22
  negative effects of, 60
  for rheumatoid arthritis, 23
  safe use of, 66
  side effects of, 63–65
  use of, 44, 61–66
  for week to two week periods, 13
  for Wobbler's Syndrome, 19
Cosequin/Cosequin-DS (Nutramax), 111, 120
COX enzymes, 60, 70–71
Cruciate injuries, 3
CT scans, 49, 50
  for cauda equina syndrome, 19
  for disk disease, 18
  for Wobbler's Syndrome, 19
Cucumaria frondosa, 107–108

Curcumin, 133
Cushing's disease, 185, 195
Cyclooxygenase, 70
Cysteine, 98
Cytotec, 82

Dachshunds, 17–18
Dallas Morning News, vii
Dancing Doberman disease, 37
Dancing Paws, 121
Deer antler, 131
Definition of arthritis, 5–6
Degenerative myelopathy, 59
Dermatitis, 93
Dermatomyositis, 20, 24–25
Devil's claw, 127, 128–129, 132
Dexamethasone, 67
Diabetes
  blood tests revealing, 52
  obesity and, 184, 189
Diagnosis
  of cauda equina syndrome, 19
  of fibrocartilage embolus (FCE), 21
  of gout, 37
  of hepatozoonosis, 31–32
  of hip dysplasia, 173–176, 197–198
  of lupus, 22
  of Lyme disease, 30–31
  of mucopolysaccharidosis, 29
  obtaining, 1–3, 13
  of osteochondrosis, 34
  of panosteitis, 36
  of polymyositis/polyarthritis, 25
  of rheumatoid arthritis, 23
  of soft tissue injuries, 16
  of thyroid disease, 25–26
  of Wobbler's Syndrome, 19
Diarrhea, 34
Diclofenac sodium, 69
Diet, 147–169. *See also* Homemade diets
  additives in processed foods, 157–160

BARF diet, 163–167
bones, dogs eating, 166
carbohydrates in processed
    foods, 156–157
chemicals in processed foods,
    160–161
contents of pet foods, 154–161
digestibility of processed foods, 162
enzymes in, 91
fat in processed foods, 156
fillers in, 148
flavorings in proceed foods, 157
generic diets, 151–152
grain products in processed
    foods, 156–157
guaranteed analysis in processed
    foods, 162
for healthy pet, 202
labels, reading, 162
natural-style diets, 152–153
nutritional adequacy of
    processed foods, 162
packaged foods, 150–153
premium foods, 152
preservatives in proccssed foods,
    157–160
proper diet, 148–150
protein in processed foods,
    154–156
raw foods, 163–167
types of, 44
weight-loss diets, 189
Diflunisal, 69
Digoxin, 77
Disk disease, 17–18
Dislocations, 15–16
Distemper vaccine, 23
Diuretics, 194–195
DMG (dimethylglycine), 116–117
DMG Vetri-Cine (Vetri-Science), 120
DMSO (dimethylsulfoxide), 117
Doberman pinschers
    Dancing Doberman disease, 37
    drug-induced joint problems,
        23–24
    Wobbler's Syndrome, 18, 28

Docosahexaenoic acid (DHA), 93
Dog Fancy magazine, viii
Dolobid, 69
Dosage
    of fatty acids, 96
    of nutritional supplements,
        89–90
    of sea cucumber jerky treat,
        108
    of shark cartilage, 110
Double-blind, placebo-controlled
    studies, 3–4
Drug-induced joint problems, 20,
    23–24
Drug treatments. See Medications
Du huo, 127
Dysplasia, 20, 29. See also specific
    types

E. coli, 167–168
EctoGesic. See Etodolac
Ehrlichiosis, 30, 53
Eicosanoids, 9, 94
Eicosapentaenoic acid (EPA), 9, 60,
    93
Elbows, 7
    dislocations, 29
    dysplasia, 3, 28
    osteochondrosis in, 34
Electrical stimulation, 179
Electroacupuncture, 134
Emulsifiers in processed foods,
    158, 160
Enalapril, 77
Enacard, 77
Endorphins, 135
Endothelial cell-stimulating angio-
    genic factor, 108–109
English sheepdogs, 28
Enkephalins, 135
Enzymes, 90–92, 169
    in barley grass, 92
    in green foods, 92–93
    in health formulas, 97–98
Epilepsy, 77

Epimedium, 131, 132
Erythema migrans, 30
Ethoxyquin (EQ), 158, 159
Etodolac, 68, 69
  cartilage damage and, 68, 69
  gastrointestinal bleeding from,
    71
  incidence of side effects, 80
  toxicity of, 82
Eucommia, 130
Evening primrose oil, 93
Exercise, 171–177
  hip dysplasia and, 175
  obesity and, 185
Exotic Pet Practice, vii

Fat in processed foods, 156
Fatty acids, xi, 9, 93–97, 169. See
    also Omega-3 fatty acids;
    Omega-6 fatty acids
  cetyl myristoleate, 118–119
  dietary ratio for, 97
  dosage of, 96
  in health formulas, 97–98
  for hip dysplasia, 176
  method for distributing, 97
  phospholipids, 94
  for soft tissue injuries, 16
  in weight-loss recipe, 191
Feldene, 69
Fenuprofen, 69
Feverfew, 129
Fibrocartilage embolus (FCE), 19, 21
Fibrosarcoma, 26
Fillers in diet, 148
Fish oils, 93
  cetyl myristoleate, 118–119
Flare-ups, 172
Flavorings in proceed foods, 157
Flax seed, 93, 95
Flea-prevention medicines
  drug-induced joint problems, 24
  informing veterinarian about,
    45–46

Fluid analysis, 53
Flunixin meglumine, 69
Flurbiprofen, 69
Folic acid, 92
Food poisoning, 164
Foods. See Diet
"4 Your Pets," vii
Fox terriers, 28
Fractures, 2–3, 15–16, 20
Free radicals, 98
  glucosamine and, 111
French bulldogs, 28
Frost, 102
Fungal bone cysts, 2
Furosemide, 77

Gamma-linolenic acid (GLA), 93
Garcinia cambogia tree, 193
Garlic
  processed foods, flavoring in, 157
  in sea cucumber jerky treat, 107
Gastrointestinal bleeding
  medications for, 82
  non-steroidal anti-inflammatories
    (NSAIDS) and, 71–72
Gauss units, 138
Generation (Vita-Flex), 120
Generic diets, 151–152
Gentiana, 131
Geriatric dogs, 14–15
  drug reactions and, 73–74
  spondylosis deformans, 36
German shepherds
  cauda equina syndrome, 28
  elbow dysplasia, 28
  panosteitis, 28, 35–36
Ginger, 129
  in Chinese herbal therapy, 131
  for weight-control, 193
Ginkgo biloba, 98
Glandular therapy, 101
  studies on, 102–103
Glass in paws, 16
Glucocorticoids. See Corticosteroids

Gluconate, 168
Glucosamine, xi, 8, 43, 110–112, 133
  acceptance of therapy, 42
  cetyl myristoleate with, 119
  Glyco-Flex Plus (Vetri-Science), 107
  manganese and, 112
  for osteochondrosis, 34
  for overuse syndrome, 32
  in sea cucumber jerky treat, 107
  side effects of, 111
  for soft tissue injuries, 16
  for spondylosis deformans, 36
Glucosamine Glycoflex/Glycoflex-
  Plus (Vetri-Science), 121
Glucosamine hydrochloride, 110
Glucosamine Multi-Source (Vetri-
  Science), 121
Glucosamine Single Source (Vetri-
  Science), 121
Glutathione
  as antioxidant, 98
Glyco-Flex Plus (Vetri-Science), 107
Glycosaminoglycans (GAGS), 8, 105
  in bovine cartilage, 106
  function of, 113
  manganese and, 112
  mucopolysaccharidosis, 29
  in perna mussels, 106–107
Gout, 20, 36–37
Grain products in processed foods,
  156–157
Grape seed extracts
  as antioxidant, 98
  bioflavonoids from, 99
Great Danes
  elbow dysplasia, 28
  Wobbler's Syndrome, 18, 28
Great Pyrenees, 28
Green foods, 92–93
Griffons, 28

Hahnemann, Samuel, 140
The Healing Power of Herbs (Murray), 133

Health formulas, 97–98
Heartworm medicines
  drug-induced joint problems,
    24
  informing veterinarian about,
    45–46
Heat intolerance, 187
Hecla lava, 144
Hematite crystals, 140
Heolen, 131
Hepatozoonosis, 20, 31–32, 53
Herbal therapies, xii, 87, 125–134
  alfalfa, 128
  boswellia, 128
  capsaicin/cayenne, 128
  Chinese herbs, guidelines for,
    126
  devil's claw, 128–129
  feverfew, 129
  ginger, 129
  horsetail, 129
  licorice, 129
  for soft tissue injuries, 16
  using, 131–134
  for weight-control, 193
  Western herbs, guidelines for,
    126
  white willow bark, 129–130
Hip dysplasia, xi, 3
  acupuncture for, 136–137
  breeds affected by, 28
  causes of, 7, 9
  checking for, 173–176, 197–198
  exercise and, 175
  surgery to correct, 84–85
  vitamin C and, 34, 99–100, 198
Hi-Potency Joint Recovery (Dancing Paws), 121
Hips, 7. See also Hip dysplasia
  joint replacement, 174–175
Histiocytosis, 26
Hobbs, R., 69, 95, 111
Holistic pet care, xii, xiv–xv, 203
  finding holistic veterinarians,
    42–45

Holistic pet care *(continued)*
 non-steroidal anti-inflammatories
  (NSAIDS) in, 80–83
 veterinarians practicing, 41–46
Homemade diets, 148–149, 161–169
 preparation of, 167–169
Homeopathy, xii, 87, 140–146, 201
 common remedies, list of, 144
 over-the-counter (OTC) reme-
  dies, 145–146
 placebo effect in, 142
 safe use of, 145–146
 side effects from, 142
 use of, 203–204
Home-Prepared Dog and Cat Diets
 (Strombeck), 190–191
Hormones and obesity, 183
Horsetail, 129
Hot packs, 178
Hyaluronic acid (HA), 113
Hydrocortisone, 67
Hydroxycitric acid (HCA) for
 weight-control, 193
Hypertension and obesity, 187
Hypothyroidism. *See* Thyroid disease

Ibuprofen, 68, 69
 gastrointestinal bleeding from, 71
Immune system, 63
Immunizations for Lyme disease, 31
Indocin, 69
Indomethacin, 69
Infectious arthritis, 20, 29–32
Inflammation, 9
Innova diet, 153
Integrative therapy, xiv
Intestinal ulcers. *See* Ulcers
Irish setters, 28
Irish wolfhounds, 28
Iron, 92

Jerky treats with sea cucumber, 107
Joint capsule, 6

Joint Maintenance (Dancing Paws),
 121
Joint Rescue (Ark Naturals), 121
Joints
 components of, 6
 fluid analysis, 53
 healing of, 6
 instability of, 3
*Journal of Arthritis and Rheuma-
 tology,* 173
*Journal of the American Geriatric
 Society,* 172–173

Kelp, 169
Ketoprofen, 69
Kidney disease, 14
 fatty acids and, 93
 non-steroidal anti-inflammatories
  (NSAIDS) and, 76
 in older dogs, 74
King Charles spaniels, 28
King Pharmacy, 120
Knees, 6
 collateral ligaments, rupture of, 16
 dislocations, 28, 29
 osteochondrosis in, 34

Labels on pet foods, reading, 162
Laboratory evaluation, 48–49
Labrador retrievers
 elbow dysplasia, 28
 obesity in, 182
Lameness, 20, 37
Larger breeds
 cauda equina syndrome, 19
 dysplasia, 29
 elbow dislocations, 29
 fibrocartilage embolus (FCE), 19,
  21
 hip dysplasia, 28
 osteochondrosis, 33–35
 panosteitis, 35–36
 Wobbler's Syndrome, 18

Laser therapy, 134, 178–179
Lasix, 77
Lecithin, 107
Licorice, 129, 132
    in Chinese herbal therapy, 131
Ligamentous injuries, 3
Ligaplex I and II (Standard
    Process), 103
Linoleic acid, 93
    enzymes and, 91
Lipase, 90, 92
Liposarcoma, 26
Liver, cooked, 169
Liver disease, 14
    etodolac and, 78
    non-steroidal anti-inflammatories
        (NSAIDS) and, 76–77
    in older dogs, 74
Lock-up of limbs, 178
Low level laser therapy (LLLT),
    178–179
Lupus, 20, 21–22, 40
Lyme borelliosis, 30
Lyme disease, 20, 29–330–31, 53

Magna-therapy collars, 140
Magnesium, 92
Magnetic collars, 140
Magnetic mats, 139–140
Magnetic therapy, 87, 137–140
Manganese
    in barley grass, 92
    glucosamine and, 112
Manipulating affected limbs, 178
Massage therapy, 172, 177–178
Matrix tissue, 8
May, Christopher, 81
Medical history, taking, 46–47
Medications
    blood tests and, 52
    drug interactions, 77
    obesity and, 187
    for rheumatoid arthritis, 23
Methylprednisolone, 67

Methylsulfonylmethane (MSM),
    117–118
    Glyco-Flex Plus (Vetri-Science), 107
Minerals
    in health formulas, 97–98
    in homemade diets, 168
    in sea cucumber, 107
    Standard Process, 103
Miniature pinschers, 28
Miniature poodles, 28, 29
Misoprostol, 82
Motrin, 69
MRI scans, 49, 50
    for cauda equina syndrome, 19
    for disk disease, 18
    for osteochondrosis, 34
    for Wobbler's Syndrome, 19
Mucopolysaccharides, 107
Mucopolysaccharidosis, 20, 28, 29
Mullein, 115
Murray, Michael, 133
Muscle wasting, 178
Mustard for weight-control, 193
Myelograms, 49, 50
    for cauda equina syndrome, 19
    for disk disease, 18
    for Wobbler's Syndrome, 19

N-acetylglucosamine, 110
Nalfon, 69
Naprelan, 69
Naprosyn, 69
    toxicity of, 82
Naproxen, 68, 69
    gastrointestinal bleeding from,
        71
Natural care, xiv
Natural Health Bible for Pets, 147
*The Natural Pharmacist: Every-
    thing You Need to Know
    about Arthritis* (Hobbs &
    Bucco), 69
The Natural Pharmacy: Arthritis
    (Hobbs & Bucco), 111

Natural-style diets, 152–153
Neurological disorders, 16–21
Neurological examination of animal, 48
Neutering and obesity, 183–184
Newfoundlands, 28
Nicotinic acid, 92
Non-steroidal anti-inflammatories (NSAIDS), xiii, xv, 2, 201
  biochemistry of, 70–71
  blood tests and, 52
  cartilage damage and, 77–79
  commonly used medications, 69
  COX pathway, 60
  for disk disease, 17, 18
  drug interactions, 77
  kidney disease and, 87
  list of possible side effects, 79
  liver disease and, 76–77
  safe use of, 80–83
  SAMe compared, 122
  side effects of, 68–79
  use of, 66, 68–83
  for week to two week periods, 13
Nuprin, 69
Nutramax, 120
NutriFlex (Rx Vitamins for Pets), 121
Nutritional supplements, xi, 43, 87, 88–104, 201. See also Chondroprotective supplements; Fatty acids
  antioxidants, 98–104
  for cauda equina syndrome, 19
  for disk disease, 17, 18
  dosage of, 89–90
  enzymes, 90–92
  glandular therapy, 101
  green foods, 92–93
  for lupus, 22
  for osteochondrosis, 34
  for overuse syndrome, 32
  for panosteitis, 36
  raw foods, 101
    several supplements, use of, 89
    for soft tissue injuries, 16
    from Standard Process, 103
    use of, 203
    for weight-control, 187, 192–194
    for Wobbler's Syndrome, 19
  NutriWeightR (RxVitamins for Pets), 194

Obesity, 148, 181–188
  body composition score, 182–183
  causes of, 183–187
  commercial weight-loss diets, 189
  defined, 182
  failure of weight-control program, 195–196
  guide for weight loss, 188–196
  hip dysplasia and, 11–12
  from overfeeding, 185–187
  problems from, 187–188
  recipe for weight control, 190–191
  spaying/neutering and, 183–184
  starvation diets, 196
  supplements for weight-control, 192–194
Older dogs. See Geriatric dogs
Omega-3 fatty acids, 93
  dietary ratio for, 97
  inflammation and, 94
  for overuse syndrome, 32
  rheumatoid arthritis and, 95–96
  in sea cucumber jerky treat, 107
  for spondylosis deformans, 36
  in weight-loss recipe, 191
Omega-6 fatty acids, 9, 93
  dietary ratio for, 97
  inflammation and, 94
Omega-9 fatty acids, 93
Onion flavoring in processed foods, 157
Orthopedic examination of animal, 48

Ortolani maneuver, 174
Osteoarthritis and Cartilage, 111
Osteochondritis, 3
Osteochondrosis, 20, 33–35
    vitamin C and, 198
Osteosarcoma, 26
Our Pets products, viii
Over-the-counter (OTC) homeo-
    pathic remedies, 145–146
Overuse syndrome, 20, 32–33
Overweight. *See* Obesity
Oxidation, 98
Oyster shell, 132

Packaged foods, 150–153
Pancreatic enzymes, 90–92
Panosteitis, 20, 28, 35–36
Pantothenic acid, 92
Paralysis, 19, 21
Parasites, 52–53
    from raw diet, 164–166
Patellar dislocations, 28, 29
Paws, glass in, 16
Pekingese, 28
PennHip evaluation, 176
Periodontal disease, 12
Perna canaliculus, 106–107
Perna mussels, 43, 106–107
    Glyco-Flex Plus (Vetri-Science),
    107
Pet Care Naturally Web site, 204
Pfizer, 72, 73–76
Phenobarbital, 77
Phenylbutazone, 69
Phenylpropanolamine, 194, 195
Phospholipids, 9, 94
Physical therapy, 177–179
Pills, 108
Piroxicam, 68, 69
    SAMe compared, 122
    toxicity of, 82
Pituitary gland, 62
Plant enzymes, 90–92
Polyarthritis, 20, 25

Polymyositis, 20, 25
Pomeranians
    atlantoaxial dislocation, 28
    shoulder dislocation, 28
Poodles, 28
Potassium, 92
Prednisolone, 67
Prednisone, 67
Premium foods, 152
Preservatives in processed foods,
    157–160
Proanthocyanidins, 99
Processed dog foods, 150–153
Prosamine (Virbac), 121
Prostaglandins, 71–72
    bioflavonoids and, 99
    non-steroidal anti-inflammatories
    (NSAIDS) and, 68
Proteases, 92
Protein
    in barley grass, 92
    in processed foods, 154–156
Proteoglycans, 8
    corticosteroids and, 63
    SAMe and, 122
PSGAG therapy
    for osteochondrosis, 34
    for soft tissue injuries, 16
Pulsatilla, 144
Pulsed electromagnetic field mag-
    nets (PEMF), 138
Puppies
    hip dysplasia in, 197
    obesity in, 186–187
    osteochondrosis, 33–35
Pycnogenol, 98–99

Radiographs, xi, 49–51, 202
    cancer, 27
    for diagnosis, 3
    for hepatozoonosis, 31
    for osteochondrosis, 34
    for panosteitis, 36
    for soft tissue injuries, 16

Radiographs *(continued)*
 for spondylosis deformans, 36
 for Wobbler's Syndrome, 19
Raw foods, 101, 163-167
 E. coli, 167-168
 glandular preparations, 103
 phytochemicals in, 102
 Salmonella, 167-168
Rectal bleeding, 78
Rehmannia, 130
Research
 complementary therapies, 3-5
 double-blind, placebo-controlled
  studies, 3-4
 on herbal therapies, 127-128, 132
 on homeopathic remedies, 143
Restaurant grease, 156
Rheumatoid arthritis, 20, 22-23
 omega-3 fatty acids and, 95-96
Rheumatoid factor (RF) blood test,
 23
Rhodesian ridgebacks, 28
Rhus toxicodendron, 144
Rice, 97-98
Richardson, Daniel, 99-100, 198
Rimadyl. *See* Carprofen
Rocky Mountain spotted fever, 30, 53
Rottweilers, 40
Rx Vitamins for Pets, 121

Saint Bernards, 28
Salfex, 69
Salicin, 129-130
Salmon, 93
Salmonella, 167-168
Salsalate, 69
SAMe (S-adenosylmethionine), 119,
 122-123
 cost of, 123
Scurvy, 102, 151
Sea cucumber, 107-108
Sea kelp
 in health formulas, 97-98
 in sea cucumber jerky treat, 107

Selenium, 91
Shark cartilage, 43, 106, 108-110
 dosage for, 110
Shelties. *See* Shetland sheepdogs
Shetland sheepdogs
 dermatomyositis, 24-25
 hip dysplasia, 28
 overuse syndrome, 32-33
Shoulders, 6
 dislocation, 28, 29
 dysplasia, 3
 osteochondrosis in, 34
Side effects
 from acupuncture, 135-136
 of carprofen, 58-59, 73-76
 of corticosteroids, 63-65
 of glucosamine, 111
 of glycosaminoglycans (GAGS),
  113
 from homeopathy, 142
 of non-steroidal anti-inflammatories (NSAIDS), 68-79
 of SAMe, 122
Skin
 dermatomyositis, 24-25
 staphylococcal pyoderm, 11-12
 thyroid disease and, 13
Skullcap, 115
Slaughterhouse wastes, 155-156
Smaller breeds
 atlantoaxial dislocation, 29
 disk disease and, 17
 patellar dislocations, 29
Soft tissue injuries, 16, 20
Solid Gold diet, 153
Solu-DeltaR, 67
Spaying and obesity, 183-184
Spine, 7
 cauda equina syndrome, 19
 causes of arthritis, 9
 disk disease, 17-18
 Wobbler's Syndrome, 18-19
Spirulina, 92-93
Splitting technique, 157
Spondylosis deformans, 20, 36

Standard Process, 103
Staphylococcal pyoderm, 11-12
Steatitis, 151
Strazza, Michael, 139
Strombeck, D. R., 190-191
Sulfa drugs, 23-24
Sulindac, 69
Superoxide dismutase, 98
Surgery, 53-54
    for arthritis, 83-85
    for cauda equina syndrome, 19
    for disk disease, 17, 18
    for hip dysplasia, 84-85
    for Wobbler's Syndrome, 19
Swimming, 172
    hip dysplasia and, 175
Syno-Flex (Vetri-Science), 121
Synovial fluid, 105
Synovial membrane, 6
Systemic lupus erythematosus
    (SLE), 21-22

Tagamet, 82
Tamarind citrus fruit, 193
Tang kuei, 127, 130
*Textbook of Veterinary Internal
    Medicine, 4th ed.* (Richard-
    son), 99-100
*Textbook of Veterinary Internal
    Medicine* (Bennett & May), 81
Thiamine deficiency in cats, 151
Thorns, 16
Thymex (Standard Process), 103
Thyroid disease, 13, 20, 25-26
    obesity and, 184, 189
Ticks. *See also* Lyme disease
    blood tests and, 52-53
    hepatozoonosis, 31-32
Tolectin, 69
Tolmetin sodium, 69
Toy breeds, 28
Trauma, 15-16, 20
    osteochondrosis, 33
Trepang, 107

Triamcinolone, 67
Trout, 93
Tuhuo Angelica, 130
Tumors, 2. *See also* Cancer
    abdominal tumors, 185
Tylenol, 68

Ulcers, 14
    medications for, 82
    non-steroidal anti-inflammatories
        (NSAIDS) and, 68, 70-71
Ultra-Flex (Vitality Systems), 121
Ultrasound, 179
Underfeeding pets, 186
Urate crystal formation, 36-37
Urine testing, 202-203

Vaccine-induced immune disor-
    ders, 20, 24
Vegetables in weight-loss diet, 192
Vertebrae. *See* Spine
Vet-A-Mix, 120
Veterinarians
    examination by, 47-48
    information to give, 45-46
    laboratory evaluation, 48-49
    medical history, taking, 46-47
    questions to ask, 44
    visits to, 39-55
Veterinary Forum, vii
Vetri-Science, 120, 121
Vetri-Shark (Vetri-Science), 121
Virbac, 121
Vita-Flex, 120
Vitality Systems, 121
Vitamin A
    as antioxidant, 98
    in barley grass, 92
Vitamin B_1, 92
Vitamin B_2, 92
Vitamin B_6
    in barley grass, 92
    enzymes and, 91

Vitamin C
  as antioxidant, 98
  in barley grass, 92
  hip dysplasia and, 99–100, 198
  in homemade diets, 168
  osteochondrosis and, 34
  for overuse syndrome, 32
  pycnogenol and, 99
  raw food products for, 101
  scurvy and, 102
Vitamin E
  as antioxidant, 98
  in barley grass, 92
  in homemade diets, 168
  in sea cucumber jerky treat, 107
Vitamins
  aquapuncture, 134
  enzymes and, 91
  green foods and, 92
  in health formulas, 97–98
  natural vitamins, 101
  in sea cucumber, 107
  Standard Process, 103
Voltaren, 69
Vomiting, 15
VPS, 120
VRx, 120

Wandering Bi syndrome, 127
Web sites
  Animal Protection Institute Web
    site, 154

Pet Care Naturally Web site,
    204
  www.planetpets.com, viii
Weight. See Obesity
Weimaraners, 28
Western herbal therapy, 126–127
  guidelines for, 126
Wheat grass, 97–98
White peony, 131, 132
White willow bark, 129–130, 132
Willow bark, 127
Wirehaired fox terriers, 28
Wobbler's Syndrome, 18–29
  breeds affected by, 28
  www.planetpets.com, viii
Wylie News, vii
Wysong diet, 153

X-rays, 49–50. See also Radio-
    graphs
  for cauda equina syndrome, 19

Yorkshire terriers
  atlantoaxial dislocation, 28
  shoulder dislocation, 29
Yucca, 115–116, 132

Zinc
  in barley grass, 92
  enzymes and, 91